DK EYEWITNESS

TOP 10
MUNICH

Top 10 Munich Highlights

The Top 10 of Everything

CONTENTS

Munich Area by Area

Streetsmart

Within each Top 10 list in this book, no hierarchy of quality or popularity is implied. All 10 are, in the editor's opinion, of roughly equal merit.

Title page, front cover and spine *Rococo-style Steinerner Saal in Schloss Nymphenburg*
Back cover, clockwise from top left *Gingerbread hearts; Carousel at Oktoberfest; Wendelstein, Bavarian Alps; Steinerner Saal; Neues Rathaus*

The rapid rate at which the world is changing is constantly keeping the DK Eyewitness team on our toes. While we've worked hard to ensure that this edition of Munich is accurate and up-to-date, we know that opening hours alter, standards shift, prices fluctuate, places close and new ones pop up in their stead. So, if you notice we've got something wrong or left something out, we want to hear about it. Please get in touch at **travelguides@dk.com**

Welcome to
Munich

The gateway to the Bavarian Alps, Munich is one of
Germany's most charming cities. Here, Baroque churches
and historic art galleries sit shoulder-to-shoulder with
lively cafés and festive beer gardens. Just beyond the centre,
fairytale castles and scenic lakes promise alpine adventure.
With DK Eyewitness Top 10 Munich, it's yours to explore.

Munich is a city of almost 1.5 million inhabitants, and one look at its
many squares filled with bustling cafés will tell you it's a city that
enjoys the good life. Locals are spoiled for choice when it comes
to the number of green spaces in which to unwind, including the
Englischer Garten and the Isar river meadows. For fans of sport
and the great outdoors, the **Olympiapark** is a top city destination;
the Upper Bavarian **lakes** and nearby **Alps** also lie within easy reach.

Ludwig I transformed Munich into his vision of "Athens on the Isar".
Today, the city is blessed with more art institutions than ever, most
of which can be found in the **museum quarter**. This is where the
city's three **Pinakotheken** (art museums) are located, along with
its two universities. Just as importantly, Munich is Germany's
undisputed capital of beer, thanks to the brewing expertise of the
monks who settled on the Isar back in the 13th century. It plays
host to the annual **Oktoberfest** and to countless **beer gardens**.

Whether you're visiting for a weekend or a week, our Top 10 guide
brings together the best of everything that Munich has to offer,
from its **Deutsches Museum** of science to the vast **Olympiapark**.
The guide has useful tips throughout, from seeking out what's
free to getting off the beaten track, plus nine easy-to-follow
itineraries, designed to tie together a clutch of sights in a short
space of time. Add inspiring photography and detailed maps,
and you've got the essential pocket-sized travel companion.
Enjoy the book, and enjoy Munich.

Clockwise from top: **Staatstheater am Gärtnerplatz, Hofbräuhaus, Olympiapark, Schloss
Nymphenburg, a Residenz lion, Oktoberfest ride**

Exploring Munich

Whether it's sightseeing, shopping or simply savouring the atmosphere, Munich has everything you're looking for and more. The old town and the Englischer Garten can be seen in just a couple of days, while those with more time to spare can also add Nymphenburg and Olympiapark to the list. These itineraries are designed to help you pack in as many of the city's highlights as possible.

The mushroom water fountains by Frauenkirche – a popular place to cool off in summer.

Key

— Two-day itinerary

— Four-day itinerary

Two Days in Munich

Day ❶
MORNING

Start the day at Frauenkirche (see pp14–15). Be sure to make your way to Marienplatz (see pp12–13) by 11am to experience the famous Glockenspiel chiming clock. Next, head to Peterskirche (see pp78–9) and climb the tower for a breathtaking view of the city. Round off the morning with a stroll at Viktualienmarkt (see p80).

AFTERNOON

Visit St-Jakobs-Platz to take in the synagogue and the Münchner Stadtmuseum (see p80) before heading over to Asamkirche (see pp80–81). From here, amble across Marienhof to take in the Staatsoper (see p89) and Residenz (see pp16–17).

Day ❷
MORNING

Make a start at Odeonsplatz (see p12), where you'll find the Theatinerkirche (see p91) and Feldherrnhalle (see p90), before making a turn into the Hofgarten (see p17). Passing through the garden, you'll reach the Haus der Kunst (see p104), and outside you'll find the famous Eisbach surfers navigating the icy waters of the stream.

AFTERNOON

Spend the afternoon in Munich's main park, the Englischer Garten (see pp22–3), and make a pit stop at the Chinesischer Turm or Seehaus.

Four Days in Munich

Day ❶
MORNING

Start in Marienplatz (see pp12–13) and take in everything it has to offer: Viktualienmarkt (see p80), Sendlinger Straße and Kaufinger Straße, all the way to the Frauenkirche (see pp14–15).

AFTERNOON

Head to Feldherrnhalle (see p90) in Odeonsplatz (see p12), and then the Theatinerkirche (see p91). Make your way to the the Residenz (see pp16–17) and then visit the Hofgarten.

Two-Piece Reclining Figure: Points is a bronze monumental sculpture created in 1969–70 by English sculptor Henry Moore. It is one of the most important of the sculptures surrounding the Pinakotheken.

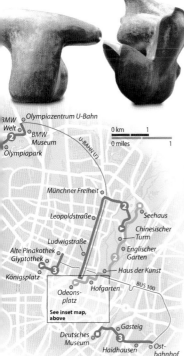

The Lenbachhaus once belonged to painter Franz von Lenbach and is now home to a collection of works by the "Blue Rider" group.

Day ❷
MORNING
Start with a stroll in the **Englischer Garten** (see pp22–3), then head to **Münchner Freiheit** (see p104) via Feilitzschstraße. Walk down **Leopoldstraße** (see p104), **Ludwigstraße** (see p97) and **Siegestor** (see p97), passing Borofsky's *Walking Man* (see p106) and **Bayerische Staatsbibliothek** (see p103).
AFTERNOON
Once you reach **Odeonsplatz** (see p12), take the U3 to Olympiazentrum. Here you can visit the **BMW Museum** (see p128) and **BMW Welt** (see p129), and take in the fascinating architecture of **Olympiapark** (see pp32–3).

Day ❸
MORNING
Start at **Königsplatz** (see p97) for a day of museums, where you're spoiled for choice with the **Glyptothek** (see p97), the **Staatliche** **Antikensammlungen** (see p97), **Städtische Galerie im Lenbachhaus** (see p97), the **Alte Pinakothek** (see pp18–19) and its sister branches, **Museum Brandhorst** (see p98) and the **Staatliches Museum Ägyptischer Kunst** (see p98).
AFTERNOON
Take bus 100 to Ostbahnhof and stroll through **Haidhausen** (see p113) with its vast selection of shops and public spaces. Next, head past **Gasteig** (see p112) to reach the **Deutsches Museum** (see pp26–9).

Day ❹
Visit the **Schloss Nymphenburg** (see pp30–31), a historic palace with extensive grounds and pavilions. When you're ready for a break, the **Schlosscafé im Palmenhaus** (see p130) is a great place to refuel. Afterwards, stop in at the **Botanischer Garten** (see p127) and end the day in the nearby **Hirschgarten** (see p128).

Top 10 Munich Highlights

Neuschwanstein, a fairy tale castle set amid the dramatic Bavarian landscape

🔟 Munich Highlights

Munich is Germany's third-largest city, and before the fall of the Berlin Wall it was dubbed the "unofficial capital of the country". Not only does it feature historical buildings, museums filled with treasures and a thriving cultural landscape, it also offers an abundance of recreational activities and a laid-back atmosphere.

① Around Marienplatz

Marienplatz is home to the Neues Rathaus and its famous Glockenspiel chiming clock (see pp12–13).

Frauenkirche ②

The domes of this Gothic cathedral – also known as the Münchner Dom – became the model for Baroque onion domes throughout Bavaria (see pp14–15).

③ Residenz

Dating back to 1385, the Residenz has been expanded by various wings and courtyards over the centuries (see pp16–17).

Alte Pinakothek ④

The three Pinakotheken can be found in the museum quarter. The oldest of these, the Alte Pinakothek (1836), houses priceless works of art (see pp18–21).

⑤ Englischer Garten

Munich's main green space is one of the largest inner-city parks in the world and a popular spot to unwind for locals and tourists alike (see pp22–3).

⑧ Olymp

EBENAU
LEONROD-PLATZ
LANDSHUTER ALLEE
LEONRODSTR.
DACHAU
PLATZ DER FREIHEIT
⑦ NYMPHENBURGER STRAS
3 km (2 miles)
MARSFELD
MARS-PLATZ 4
ARNULFSTRASSE
LANDSBERGER STRASSE
SCHWANTHALER-HÖHE
THERESIENHÖHE
⑨ Theresien wiese

6 Deutsches Museum

Pulling in more than 1.5 million visitors every year, this institution is the world's oldest and largest museum of science and technology and not to be missed (see pp26–9).

7 Schloss Nymphenburg

This summer palace from 1664 was once situated outside the city. Its extensive grounds make it a green oasis in west Munich (see pp30–31).

Around Munich

Landsberg am Lech · Munich · Grünwald · Starnberg · Schäftlam · Ammersee · Dießen · Starnberger See · Geretsried · Wessobrunn · Peißenberg · Seeshaupt · Penzberg · Bad Tölz · Steingaden · Rottenbuch · Murnau · Kochel am See · Ettal · Linderhof

0 km 20
0 miles 20

8 Olympiapark

The tent-style construction of the Olympic Stadium (1972) was an innovative feat of architecture when it was first built and it's still worth a visit today (see pp32–3).

9 Oktoberfest

Every year millions of visitors flock to the largest beer festival in the world (see pp34–5).

Neuschwanstein 10

Ludwig II's most famous castle was inspired by his admiration for Wagner operas (see pp36–7).

🔟 ⭐ Around Marienplatz

Marienplatz has been the heart of Munich for centuries and is still the most popular place in the city to meet up or start a walking tour. The square is dominated by the Neues Rathaus (New Town Hall), which serves as a backdrop to the Mariensäule (Column of the Virgin Mary) and Fischbrunnen (Fish Fountain). Head west of the square to reach the start of the pedestrian zone, north for Weinstraße and Theatinerstraße, east for the Isartor gate and Maximilianstraße, and south to reach Viktualienmarkt.

2 Neues Rathaus

The Neo-Gothic town hall **(right)** was built between 1867 and 1909. At the top of the tower (see p79) sits the city mascot, the Münchner Kindl (Munich Child), while the famous Glockenspiel chiming clock show takes place daily in its alcoves.

3 Dallmayr

Behind the town hall once stood the green oasis of Marienhof. It has now become the site of an S-Bahn station. The impressive yellow-and-white façade on the right belongs to the well-known foodie paradise of Dallmayr (see p93).

1 Altes Rathaus

This Gothic building **(above)** dates back to 1470 and is situated in the eastern corner of Marienplatz. The Altes Rathaus (see p79) features both a grand hall and a tower (formerly the gateway to the city). It is home to a toy museum, which houses a selection of antique toys.

4 Peterskirche

Munich's oldest parish church (see p42), Peterskirche sits atop the highest point in the old town. Its Renaissance tower, known as "Alter Peter" (Old Pete), is one of the city's best-known landmarks.

5 Odeonsplatz

A wander around Odeonsplatz shows why Munich is sometimes called "Italy's northernmost city". The square is bordered by the Italianate, late Baroque Theatinerkirche (see p91), the Residenz, the Hofgarten and its archways, and Feldherrnhalle **(left)**, built in 1844 by Friedrich von Gärtner, who drew inspiration from the Florentine Loggia dei Lanzi.

6 Viktualienmarkt

This daily food market *(see p80)* originated in 1807, and a stroll through its 140 stalls is a real must. The southernmost end is home to Der Pschorr and the Schrannenhalle, which offer a wide variety of Italian delicacies.

Around Marienplatz

7 Sendlinger Straße

This shopping district *(see p70)* has two main attractions – the late Baroque Asamkirche and, right next door, the Asam-Haus with its impressive façade *(see pp80–81)*.

9 Pedestrian Zone

Munich's most popular traffic-free shopping zone *(see p70)* starts to the west of Marienplatz and extends through to Karlsplatz. This is also the location of the late Renaissance Michaelskirche *(see p42)*.

10 National-theater

Located next door to the Residenz, the Nationaltheater **(above)** is one of the largest opera stages in the world. This temple-like structure *(see p89)* has been destroyed and rebuilt twice in its lifetime.

8 Residenz

Max-Joseph-Platz is the site of the 130-room Residenz *(see pp16–17)*, a palace that functioned as a home to the Bavarian monarchs for five centuries. The buildings date back to 1385, when the Neuveste was built in the part of Munich enclosed by city walls. Its monumental façades and courtyards are open to the public, and the Residenz-museum is housed inside.

NEED TO KNOW

MAP N3–4
■ S1–S8: Marienplatz, U3/U6: Marienplatz and Odeonsplatz

Altes Rathaus:
Toy Museum: (089) 294 001; open10am–5:30pm daily; adm €6, concessions €2

Neues Rathaus:
(089) 2339 6555; tours: 3:30pm Mon & Fri, 11:30am & 1:30pm Sat; adm €18, concessions €12, under-18s free;

Tower: open 10am–7pm Mon–Fri (winter: until 5pm); adm €6, under-6s free

Glockenspiel chiming clock show: 11am & noon daily (Mar–Oct: also at 5pm)

Peterskirche:
(089) 2 1023 7760; Tower: open 9am–7pm Mon–Fri, 10am–7pm Sat & Sun (winter: until 6pm); adm €5, concessions €3

🔟 ⭐ Frauenkirche

The Frauenkirche – or, more formally, Dom zu Unserer Lieben Frau (Cathedral of Our Dear Lady) – is the largest Gothic hall church in southern Germany. It was built between 1468 and 1488 by Jörg von Halspach and Lucas Rottaler to replace an earlier Romanesque church. The domes atop its two almost 100-m (328-ft) towers, dominate the city's skyline – no buildings are permitted to be built higher.

The Devil's Footprint ①

This footprint **(right)**, complete with a spur at the heel, is said to have been made by the devil after losing a bet with the cathedral's builders.

② Bridal Doorway

The southeastern entrance is adorned with delicate figurines and other elaborate embellishments.

④ Choir Carvings

The choir stalls and screens in the chancel display figures and reliefs added between 1495 and 1502 by Erasmus Grasser.

⑤ Vaulted Ceilings

The original vaulted ceiling **(left)**, with its star pattern, was destroyed in World War II, and meticulously restored in 1990–93.

The Emperor's Tomb ③

The intricately carved tomb of Emperor Ludwig IV of Bavaria **(right)** was completed in 1622 by Hans Krumpper.

6 Organ

The main organ **(above)** is one of four in the cathedral and was built by Georg Jann in 1994. It is a gigantic instrument, with tubes ranging in size from drainpipes to straws.

7 Memminger Altar

From the chancel to the right and left of the Mariensäule (column), it is possible to see parts of the winged Memminger Altar, designed in around 1500 by Claus Strigel.

8 Cathedral Windows

The windows **(left)** were added at various times over the centuries. Some of the original Gothic and stained-glass windows are still *in situ*.

9 Statue of St Christopher

This figure, carved in around 1525, exemplifies the dramatic style of the late Gothic period.

10 Towers

The two towers, with their Renaissance domes **(above)**, were modelled on the Dome of the Rock in Jerusalem. Only the South Tower can be climbed by visitors.

NEED TO KNOW

MAP M3 ■ Frauenplatz ■ S-Bahn and U-Bahn: Marienplatz ■ (089) 21791 ■ www.muenchner-dom.de

Open 8am–8pm Mon–Sat, (from 9:30am Sun)

Guided tours: May–Sep: 3pm Tue, Thu & Sun (€7.50); no tours during Mass (9am, noon & 5:30pm Mon–Sat, 10am Sun)

Towers: South tower: open 10am–5pm Mon–Sat, 11:30am–5pm Sun

■ The cathedral hosts organ concerts, choir performances and various other recitals.

■ In addition to standard tours, there are themed tours such as one on the cathedral windows.

■ The cathedral shop is a good place to visit for souvenirs.

■ There are fountains between Frauenplatz and Augustinerstraße, offering respite for tired feet.

Frauenkirche Guide
The church houses one of Germany's most important bell collections – five from the Middle Ages and two from the Baroque period.

Residenz

Located in the heart of the city, this former residence of Bavarian kings, home to the Wittelsbach dynasty until 1918, began in 1385 as a moated castle, but grew over the centuries into an extensive complex with ten courtyards. The largest city-centre castle in Germany, it exhibits a mishmash of styles, from the Baroque Cuvilliés-Theater to the Mannerist Reiche Kapelle. Tours are self-guided, so you can take your time exploring the many interiors open to the public.

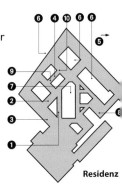

Residenz

① Antiquarium
Commissioned by Duke Albrecht V, this 69-m (226-ft) long vault **(above)** is embellished with allegorical frescoes, grotesque paintings and Bavarian landscapes.

② Grüne Galerie
The Reiches Zimmer suite, designed by François Cuvilliés the Elder, is home to the Green Gallery **(left)**, in which Elector Karl Albrecht hosted a great many parties.

③ Schatzkammer
The 16th-century treasury contains the Wittelsbach dynasty's crown jewels, gold reliquaries, porcelain and other treasures.

④ Hofkapelle
This elaborately stuccoed, two-storey chapel was built in 1601–14 by Hans Krumpper. Courtiers would congregate down below, while the ruling family would attend Mass from the upper galleries.

8 Cuvilliés-Theater

This theatre (left), built by François Cuvilliés the Elder in 1751–5, is considered the most beautiful Rococo theatre in Europe. It once staged magnificent Baroque operas and is still used today for performances of all kinds.

5 Hofgarten

Shaded by linden trees on the north side of the Residenz, this Renaissance garden, dating back to 1613, exudes a southern European air. The Temple of Diana, designed by Heinrich Schön the Elder, stands at the heart of the garden's network of pathways.

7 Lions

The front of the Residenz building is guarded by four bronze lions bearing shields (left). All of their muzzles are worn down, which is due to the local tradition of stroking them for good luck when passing by.

9 Reiche Kapelle

With its ebony altar, coloured marble and gilded reliefs, Maximilian I's elaborate private chapel (1607) is a prime example of Mannerist architecture.

10 Staatliche Münzsammlung

This museum is home to the world's largest collection of coins, alongside banknotes, medals and cut stones, including antique gems.

6 Inner Courtyards

Of the various courtyards, look out for the Grottenhof (right) and the octagonal-shaped Brunnenhof. The largest courtyard is the Apothekenhof, while the one by Cuvilliés-Theater is the smallest.

NEED TO KNOW

MAP N3 ▪ Residenzstraße 1 ▪ U3/U6 & U4/U5: Odeonsplatz ▪ (089) 290 671 ▪ www.residenz-muenchen.de

Residenz: open Apr–mid-Oct: 9am–6pm daily; mid-Oct–Mar: 10am–5pm daily; closed 1 Jan, Shrove Tue, 24, 25 & 31 Dec; wheelchair users may have to be accompanied by a member of staff; adm €9, concessions €8; combined museum/Schatzkammer ticket €14, concessions €12, under-18s free; audio guide available

Cuvilliés-Theater: open Apr–mid-Oct: 2–6pm Mon–Sat, 9am–6pm Sun & public holidays (Aug–mid-Sep: from 9am daily); mid-Oct–Mar: 2–5pm Mon–Sat, 10am–5pm

Sun & public holidays; adm €5, concessions €4

Staatliche Münzsammlung: Residenzstraße 1 (entrance on Kapellen-hof); (089) 227 221; open 10am–5pm Tue–Sun; adm €3, concessions €2, Sun €1, under-18s free; www.staatliche-muenzsammlung.de

▪ Some of the Residenz rooms are likely to be closed for renovation.

🔟 ⭐ Alte Pinakothek

Munich's Pinakotheken, three top-class art galleries, are located in the museum quarter. The Alte Pinakothek was founded by Ludwig I, designed by Leo von Klenze, and opened in 1836. The Pinakothek der Moderne and Neue Pinakothek complete the trio. The Alte Pinakothek houses collections of Bavarian dukes, electors and kings, as well as the treasures of dissolved monasteries. Completely renovated to make it more energy efficient, the museum was reopened in 2019 with optimized lighting for a better visitor experience.

1 El Greco's *Disrobing of Christ*

El Greco created this sombre work **(above)** in 1580–95. It forms part of an exceptional collection of Spanish paintings.

4 Dürer's *Four Apostles*

The gallery's Dürer collection documents his development from *Self-Portrait in Fur Coat* (1500) to the *Four Apostles* (1526), painted two years before his death.

2 Titian's *Portrait of Charles V*

Titian painted this portrait of Charles V when the emperor visited the imperial court at Augsburg in 1548.

3 Rubens' *The Rape of the Daughters of Leucippus*

In this high Baroque masterpiece **(right)** dating from 1618, Rubens depicts a mythical tangle of human and horse.

5 Rembrandt's *Descent from the Cross*

Dramatic lighting characterizes the artist's 1633 masterpiece, which was a stark contrast to the idealized representations of Christ typical of the time. The figure in blue is a self-portrait.

6 Hals' *Willem van Heythuysen*

Frans Hals' painting **(right)** of the Haarlem cloth merchant is an outstanding example of Dutch portraiture.

7 Altdorfer's *Battle of Alexander at Issus*

Albrecht Altdorfer's 1529 painting **(left)** depicts the decisive moment of Alexander the Great's victory over the Persian King Darius.

8 Holbein's *Presentation of Jesus at the Temple*

This late Gothic piece (1502) by Hans Holbein the Elder forms part of the Kaisheim altar.

9 Brueghel's *Land of Cockaigne*

Pieter Brueghel the Elder, the most significant artist of the Flemish School, offers a satirical depiction of gluttony and idleness in this painting **(left)** from 1567, which is based on a tale by Hans Sachs.

10 Botticelli's *Lamentation of Christ*

Sandro Botticelli's painting from around 1490 is renowned for its red tones, stark contrasts and curved lines. It is considered one of the great masterpieces of Italian Renaissance painting.

NEED TO KNOW

MAP F3–F4/M2
▪ Barer Straße 27
▪ (089) 2380 5216
▪ U2: Theresienstraße, Tram 27, Bus 100
▪ www.pinakothek.de

Open 10am–8:30pm Tue & Wed, 10am–6pm Thu–Sun

Adm €7, concessions €5, €1 on Sun

Pinakothek der Moderne: Barer Straße 40; (089) 2380 5360; open 10am–8pm Thu, 10am–6pm Tue, Wed & Fri–Sun; adm €10, concessions €7, €1 on Sun

Museum Brandhorst: Theresienstraße 35a; (089) 23805 2286; open 10am–6pm Tue–Sun (until 8pm Thu); adm €7, concessions €5, €1 on Sun; www.museum brandhorst.de

▪ Check the website for information about combined tickets, audio guides and tours.

▪ The Alte Pinakothek, Pinakothek der Moderne and Museum Brandhorst all have cafés and museum shops.

Museum Guide

The Alte Pinakothek, Neue Pinakothek and Pinakothek der Moderne are within walking distance of one another in the Museum Quarter. As the Neue Pinakothek is currently closed for renovation and will reopen in 2025, some of the museum's masterpieces are temporarily housed at the Alte Pinakothek. The Museum Brandhorst also features a world-class collection of modern art.

Pinakothek der Moderne

1 The Classic Modern Collection

The Classic Modern encompasses the period from the early 20th century up to 1960 and features works by Kirchner, Nolde, Braque, Picasso, Klee and Beckmann among others.

2 Surrealism

The Surrealist pieces in the museum come from the Wormland collection. Among the highlights are Salvador Dalí's *The Enigma of Desire* (1929) and Max Ernst's *Fireside Angel* (1937).

3 The Contemporary Art Collection

This section documents the art scene from 1960 onwards and includes works by de Kooning, Bacon, Beuys, Baselitz, Polke, Warhol, Flavin, Wall and Twombly.

4 The Design Museum

Modern utilitarian objects are the theme of this 80,000-strong collection at Die Neue Sammlung – The Design Museum. The exhibits

here range from Thonet chairs and Pop furniture right through to objects from the world of aerodynamics and digital culture.

5 Installations

Permanent installations at the museum include Joseph Beuys' *The End of the Twentieth Century* (1983) and works from Dan Flavin's *'monuments' for V. Tatlin* (1964).

6 The Graphic Arts Collection

This collection comprises tens of thousands of drawings and prints, though only a fraction is ever on display at any one time. Highlights include works by Old Masters such as Rembrandt and Michelangelo, in addition to pieces by Cézanne, Baselitz and Wols.

7 Drawings

Among the highlights of this collection are Raphael's red chalk drawing of *Mercury and Psyche* (1517/18) and Franz Marc's *The Tower of Blue Horses* (1912) in ink.

8 The Architecture Collection

Some 350,000 drawings and plans, 100,000 photographs and 500 models are presented in rotating exhibits on the ground floor.

9 Drawings and Sketches

With a firm focus on German architecture from the 18th to the 21st centuries, these exhibits include drawings and sketches by Balthasar Neumann, Leo von Klenze and Le Corbusier.

10 Design Vision

This two-storey display cabinet showcases objects that illuminate the full spectrum of the gallery's collection, ranging from visionary ideas through to everyday objects.

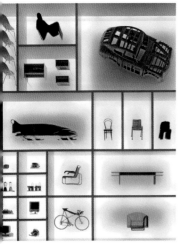

Exhibits in The Design Museum

Museum Brandhorst

The colourful *Lepanto* cycle by Cy Twombly at Museum Brandhorst

1 Warhol's *Self-Portrait*
The Brandhorst has over 100 works by Andy Warhol, making this the biggest collection of its kind in Europe. His *Self-Portrait* (1986) is almost always on display, as are his pop-art Marilyn Monroe images.

Museum Brandhorst at sundown

2 Hirst's *In This Terrible Moment*
In This Terrible Moment (2002), one of Damien Hirst's most powerful works, is a permanent fixture here.

3 Flavin's 'monuments' for V. Tatlin
Light artist Dan Flavin illuminates sections of the museum with fluorescent tubes. A work from his famed *'monuments' for V. Tatlin* (1964–82) series is always on display.

4 Koon's *Amore*
Jeff Koon's *Amore* (1988) is a small porcelain sculpture with an "I Love You" sticker and Rococo base.

5 Twombly's *Lepanto*
American painter Cy Twombly is big among fans of contemporary art – his *Lepanto* (2011) cycle is representative of his style involving splashing paint onto canvas.

6 Polke's *Liberté, Égalité, Fraternité*
The museum features many works by German artist Sigmar Polke, including one of his best-known works *Liberté, Égalité, Fraternité* (1988).

7 Katz's *The Black Dress*
Alex Katz's *The Black Dress* (1960) depicts various women in the same black dress and is considered one of his most important works.

8 Noland's *Tanya as a Bandit*
Cady Noland's aluminium replica of an image of Patty Hearst (1989) examines the sensational nature of the press.

9 Wool's *Kidnapped*
Christopher Wool's *Kidnapped* (1994) is typical of his paintings, which are often post-pop-art graffiti works created on aluminium sheets.

10 Chamberlain's *Lilith*
The Brandhorst features both paintings and sculptures by John Chamberlain. A group of mangled metal figures called *Lilith* (1967–68) is his most striking work here.

🔟 ⭐ Englischer Garten

One of the largest inner-city parks in Europe, the Englischer Garten was conceived by Sir Benjamin Thompson (1753–1814), who was awarded the title of Count Rumford by Karl Theodor, Elector of Bavaria. As Bavarian minister of war and a social reformist, Rumford ordered that the marshy banks of the Isar be converted into a park, initially for the use of the army, but it was opened to the public in 1792. As the park continued to grow, its design was taken over by court gardener Friedrich L von Sckell. Much expanded, it remains the green lung of Munich to this day.

1 Rumford Monument

This monument **(above)** in honour of Count Rumford was erected in 1796 by leading Bavarian sculptor Franz Jakob Schwanthaler.

2 Monopteros

This classical round temple was built in 1836 by Leo von Klenze. It sits atop an artificial hill, which is a popular spot all year round, attracting sunbathers in the summer and tobogganists in winter.

3 Kleinhesseloher See

This lake **(above)** can be found in the northernmost corner of the park. It is the perfect spot to hire a rowing boat or pedalo on the water. The shores of the lake are home to a scenic beer garden.

4 Seehaus

The beer garden belonging to the Seehaus restaurant occupies an idyllic spot on Kleinhesseloher See, partly shaded by the nearby trees. If the weather is good, it stays open out of season.

5 Orangerie

The former orangery now serves as an exhibition space.

6 Surfers on the Eisbach

Undeterred by the icy waters, surfers engage with the Eisbach rapids **(left)**, at the southernmost tip of the park.

8 Chinesischer Turm

The Chinese Tower **(left)** is one of the city's most emblematic landmarks. Standing five storeys high, the wooden pagoda in the traditional Chinese style dates back to 1789 and has burnt down and been rebuilt several times. At the foot of the tower is one of Munich's best beer gardens.

10 Historisches Karussell

Right next to the Chinesischer Turm is a Biedermeier-style children's roundabout, complete with carriages, sleighs and whimsical wooden animals. It is still in use today.

Englischer Garten

9 Japanisches Teehaus

The teahouse and its Japanese garden **(below)** can be found at the south end of the park on an artificial island in the Schwabinger Bach. This structure was built for the 1972 summer Olympic Games and is now only open for private events.

7 Friedrich-Ludwig-von-Sckell Monument

This memorial, designed by Klenze in 1824, was built in memory of the park's designer.

NEED TO KNOW

MAP H1–G4 ■ U3/U6: Odeonsplatz–Münchner Freiheit; Bus 100: Chinesischer Turm; Tram 18: Tivolistraße

Seehaus: Kleinhesseloher 3; (089) 381 6130

Orangerie: Englischer Garten 1A; only open for exhibitions

Chinesischer Turm: Englischer Garten 3; (089)

383 8730; restaurant: open all year round; beer garden: open May–Sep; brass band: Wed–Sun; folk dancing at the traditional Kocherlball: from 6am 3rd Sun Jul

Japanisches Teehaus: Königinstraße 4; (089) 224319; tea ceremony: open for private events only

Historisches Karussell: Englischer Garten 4; open

Apr–Oct: from 2pm daily (from 1pm in summer hols)

■ The Englischer Garten has four restaurants with attached beer gardens, the largest of which is located close to the Chinese Tower.

■ With 78 km (49 miles) of pathways, including 12 km (7 miles) of bridle paths, this park is perfect for cyclists and hikers.

Following pages Visitors at the Englischer Garten on a sunny day

TOP 10 ★ Deutsches Museum

The world's largest museum of technology and engineering was founded in 1903 by German engineer Oskar von Miller. It is located in a building on Museumsinsel (museum island) and currently houses around 28,000 exhibits. There are two other branches of the popular museum; the Verkehrszentrum near the Theresienwiese and the Flugwerft Schleißheim, north of the centre.

Planet trail sign

4 Planetarium
The planetarium allows visitors to get an unparalleled look at the night skies above Munich and even to step back in history. Thirty-minute shows take place here every day at noon and 2pm.

6 Power Machinery
Steam engines, motors and generators are to be found in this section. Some of these colossal machines, like the Alban high-pressure steam engine from 1839, are veritable works of art.

1 Faraday Cage
The Energy exhibit is home to a high-voltage installation **(above)**, which allows visitors to get close to electrical phenomena. Tours of the Faraday cage are perennially popular (11am, 2 & 4pm daily).

Physics 2
In the Physics section **(right)**, a recon-struction of Galileo's workshop features a collection of equipment used by the famous Italian astronomer and physicist.

3 Enigma Machine
The Enigma encoding machine built during World War II is a fine example of early infor-mation technology.

5 Marine Navigation
Along with countless model ships, the vast exhibition hall of the marine navigation section fea-tures several original historical sailboats and steam boats, such as the 1932 steam tugboat *Renzo* and the 1880 wooden fishing vessel *Ewer Maria*.

9 Mining
Split over two floors, much of the space in the Mining section (see p28) is built to resemble a real mine, creating an atmospheric exhibit.

10 Musical Instruments
Instruments here range from medieval lutes to the latest synthesizers.

7 Pharmaceuticals
The highlight of this fascinating section is a walk-through model of a human cell, the cell wall magnified 350,000 times (above). Visitors can also enjoy a presentation on genetic engineering and the development and production of modern pharmaceuticals.

8 Microelectronics
This section is home to some valuable original objects, among them the first telephone, dating from 1863, an AEG radio transmitter from 1913 and a manual switchboard from 1905.

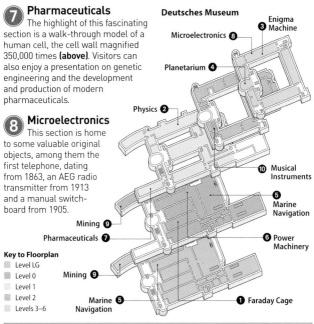

Deutsches Museum

❸ Enigma Machine
Microelectronics ❽
Planetarium ❹
Physics ❷
❿ Musical Instruments
❺ Marine Navigation
Mining ❾
Pharmaceuticals ❼
❻ Power Machinery
Mining ❾
Marine ❺ Navigation
❶ Faraday Cage

Key to Floorplan
- Level LG
- Level 0
- Level 1
- Level 2
- Levels 3–6

NEED TO KNOW

Deutsches Museum:
MAP F5; Museumsinsel 1; S1–S8: Isartor, Tram 16: Deutsches Museum; (089) 21791, (089) 217 9333; open 9am–5pm daily; closed 1 Jan, Shrove Tue, Good Fri, 1 May, 1 Nov, 24, 25 & 31 Dec; adm €14, concessions €4.50/€8, combined ticket (for Museumsinsel, Flugwerft

and Verkehrszentrum) €18; www.deutsches-museum.de

Planetarium: adm €2, evening lectures €3; tours: 2-hour highlights tour at 11am & 2pm, €3

Verkehrszentrum:
MAP J4; Am Bavariapark 5; U4/5: Schwanthaler höhe; (089) 50080 6762; open 9am–5pm daily; closed as main

museum; adm €7, concessions €3; overview tours: 11am, 1:30 & 2pm

Flugwerft Schleißheim:
Effnerstraße 18, 85764 Oberschleißheim; S1: Oberschleißheim; (089) 315 7140 ; open 9am–5pm daily; closed as main museum; adm €7, concessions €3; overview tours: 11am & 3:30pm

Deutsches Museum: Collections

 Physics and Astronomy
The Physics section features measuring and observation devices, including Foucault's pendulum. Astronomy has sections on the sun, stars and astrophysics.

 Pharmaceuticals, Chemistry and Clocks
The Clocks exhibit has examples of traditional craftsmanship on display. In Chemistry there's a reconstruction of von Liebig's laboratory, while Pharmaceuticals examines medicinal plants and drug development.

Inside the replica mine

Energy and Power Machinery
From original windmills to plasma and fusion technology, this section features inventions that make our lives easier. The huge steam engines and high-voltage experiments are not to be missed.

Tools, Ceramics and Glass
Paper and glass manufacturing, ceramics production from bricks to fine china, and tools from Stone-Age drills to computer-controlled lathes can all be found in this section.

 New Technologies
Recent research findings from climate research to nano-technology and medical technology are presented here.

 Mining, Metals and Agricultural Engineering
The spectacular mine reconstruction in this section is complemented by exhibits on the 12,000- year-old history of metallurgy. The agriculture section illustrates the cultivation of cereals and grain, and the pro-cess of brewing.

 Marine Navigation
Numerous model ships illustrate several millennia of marine navigation in this section. The rescue cruiser *Theodor Heuss* is displayed in the open-air exhibition space.

Historic Aviation
The Origins of Aviation section showcases developments from balloons and airships to the very first engine flights.

Water and Civil Engineering
An authentic suspension bridge dominates the exhibition hall, with wall-mounted screens tracking the oscillations as visitors cross over its swaying structure.

Kids' Zone
This section is brimming with interactive exhibits designed for young scientists aged three and up.

Lab inside New Technologies

BRANCHES OF THE DEUTSCHES MUSEUM

Flugwerft Schleißheim, the Deutsches Museum's branch museum on the history of aviation, is located in an old aeroplane hangar on a historic airfield in Schleißheim (see p27). In addition to the buildings and airfield itself, the site comprises 7,800 square metres (83,958 sq ft) of exhibition space, housing over 50 aeroplanes, helicopters and hang-gliders, plus various instruments and equipment.

At the Verkehrszentrum, or Transport Centre, on Theresienhöhe (see p27), three halls that were once home to the Messe München trade fair now house historic locomotives, cars, carriages and bicycles. This part of the Deutsches Museum represents the largest transport museum in the world, offering a comprehensive exploration of urban transport and travel as a whole.

FLUGWERFT AND VERKEHRSZENTRUM HIGHLIGHTS

1 Fokker D VII fighter aircraft (World War I)

2 Douglas DC-3 commercial aircraft, 1943

3 Heinkel He 111, bomber aircraft (World War II)

4 Lockheed F-104 Starfighter

5 Dornier Do 31, vertical lift-off aircraft

6 *Puffing Billy* (first locomotive in the world)

7 Drais wheel

8 Benz motor car (the first automobile in the world)

9 Rumpler "Tropfenwagen" (aerodynamic car, 1921)

10 NSU Delphin III (motorcycle, 1956)

Street scene at the Verkehrszentrum

Inside Flugwerft Schleißheim

Schloss Nymphenburg

To celebrate the birth of their son Max Emanuel in 1662, the Elector Ferdinand Maria and his wife Henriette Adelaide of Savoy commissioned Agostino Barelli to build a summer palace to the west of Munich. Building began in 1664, and the wings and annexe buildings were added from 1701 onwards. Over the course of 300 years, the original ornamental garden was expanded into a vast park comprising Baroque gardens, a system of canals, and small pavilions dotted throughout the grounds.

1 The Palace

Elector Max Emanuel and Karl Albrecht expanded the original villa **(right)** by adding buildings designed by Enrico Zuccalli and Joseph Effner. Arcaded galleries connect them to the main building.

2 Gallery of Beauties

Ludwig I commissioned court artist Joseph Stieler to create these portraits of noblewomen, townswomen and dancers, including Lola Montez **(above)**, Irish mistress of King Ludwig I.

3 Steinerner Saal

The Rococo embellishment in the ballroom was created by Johann B Zimmermann and Cuvilliés the Elder in the reign of Max III Joseph.

4 Lackkabinett

This room was designed in 1764 by Cuvilliés the Elder. Chinese black laquer motifs on wood panelling are reprised in the Rococo ceiling fresco.

6 Marstall-museum

This building houses carriages and sleighs that once belonged to the Bavarian rulers, including the gilded state coach of Ludwig II **(below)**.

5 Monopteros

Between 1804 and 1823, Friedrich L von Sckell created a landscaped park behind the palace. During this time Monopteros, the Apollo temple, was built on the Badenburger See.

Schloss Nymphenburg

7 Palace Gardens

Symmetrically designed French gardens to the rear of the palace give way to an English-style landscaped park, which was created by using the existing forest. The gardens are home to a number of individual pavilions.

9 Badenburg

Featuring a ballroom and two-storey bathing hall complete with a heated pool, this pavilion is definitely worth a visit. Three of the rooms are lined with Chinese-style wallpaper.

10 Pagodenburg

This 18th-century pavilion with an octagonal floor plan combines Western and Eastern ornamentation to stunning effect.

Amalienburg 8

Built by Cuvilliés the Elder between 1734 and 1739 for the Electress Amalia, this small hunting lodge (right) is a masterpiece of European Rococo.

NEED TO KNOW

MAP AB2–3 ■ Tram 17: Schloss Nymphenburg ■ (089) 179080 ■ Adm €8, concessions €7 ■ www.schloss-nymphenburg.de

The Palace and Marstallmuseum: open Apr–mid-Oct: 9am–6pm daily, mid-Oct–Mar: 10am–4pm daily; closed 1 Jan, Shrove Tue, 24, 25 & 31 Dec; adm; no regular tours (various themed tours available, see website); audio guides available

Palace Gardens: open Jan–Mar, Nov & Dec: 6am–6pm daily; May–Sep: 6am–9:30pm daily; Apr & Oct: 6am–8pm daily

Amalienburg , Badenburg and Pagodenburg: open Apr–mid-Oct: 9am–6pm daily; adm: €5, concessions €4

■ The Museum Mensch und Natur *(see p127)* occupies one of the wings of Schloss Nymphenburg.

■ The Schlosscafé im Palmenhaus is the perfect place to take a break from sightseeing *(open 11am–6pm daily; (089) 175309).*

TOP 10 ⭐ Olympiapark

In preparation for the 1972 Olympic Games, a former airfield and parade ground were transformed into an Olympic park, featuring hills, an artificial lake, a communications tower and sports facilities across an area measuring 3 sq km (1 sq mile). Designed by architectural firm Behnisch & Partners, the elegant, airy Olympic complex, complete with a transparent, curved, tensile roof, is still considered to be a masterpiece of modern architecture.

① BMW Welt
BMW's car delivery and exhibition centre **(below)** is the epitome of dynamism and elegance. It contains restaurants and shops and hosts events *(see p129)*.

④ Olympic Skating Rink
The skating rink is the perfect place to bring the kids on winter days. In the evening there's disco skating. Ice skates are available for hire.

② Father Timofej's Chapel
This Russian Orthodox chapel was built on the site (without a permit) in 1951 by Russian exiles Timofej and Natascha.

⑤ Kino am Olympiasee
Enjoy a summer evening at the open-air cinema **(below)** by the lake, with films often shown in their original language.

⑥ Olympiaturm
A high-speed lift transports visitors to the observation deck and revolving restaurant at the top of this 290 m (951 ft) tower **(above)**. The views across the site and city are incredible – when the Föhn winds are blowing, you can even see the Alps. The restaurant takes 49 minutes to complete a full revolution.

③ Olympic Hall
This venue holds up to 15,500 spectators beneath a section of the tensile roof, which is suspended from 58 pylons. In addition to sporting events, the hall also hosts concerts and trade fairs.

Lake and Park ⑧
Much of this site **(right)** is purpose-built, including the lake – boats can be hired in summer – and the hills, created by covering piles of war debris with turf.

⑨ Sea Life
This aquarium *(see p53)* is home to an array of underwater creatures, including seahorses, rays and tropical fish. The shark tunnel is a highlight.

⑩ Olympia-stadion
With a capacity of 69,250 spectators, the Olympic stadium is now used to host concerts and events.

Olympiapark

U Olympiazentrum

GEORG- BRAUCHLE-RING

Olympiasee

400 metres (440 yards) ②

Olympia Schwimmhalle ⑦
One of the largest in Europe, this aquatic centre **(right)** has five pools, a 10 m (33 ft) diving board, saunas, sunbathing areas, a gym and wellness features.

NEED TO KNOW

MAP D1 ■ Spiridon-Louis-Ring 21 ■ U3: Olympia-zentrum ■ (089) 3067 0 ■ www.olympiapark.de

Olympiaturm: open 9am–11pm Mon–Sat; adm: €11, concessions €7, family ticket (4 people) €23; under-6s free

Olympia Schwimmhalle: Opening hours vary, check website; www.swm.de

Olympiastadion: open 10am–8pm daily; closed 24 & 31 Dec; adm €3.50, concessions €2.50, family ticket (4 people) €8.50; stadium tour: €8, concessions €6

■ The Olympiastadion runs tours and activities based around its tensile roof, including abseiling. Prices range from €43 to €73. Call (089) 3067 2414 for more details.

■ The on-site railway takes visitors on a journey through the history of the Olympic park. Call (089) 3067 2414 or 3067 2415 for more information or tickets.

■ Theatron, Olympiapark's amphitheatre, is the venue for a number of free open-air summer concerts *(see p75)* at Whitsuntide and in the month of August.

🔟 ⭐ Oktoberfest

With around 6.5 million visitors consuming 7 million litres (12 million pints) of beer, 500,000 roast chickens and 100 oxen, Munich's Oktoberfest is the largest beer festival in the world. At the foot of the Bavaria statue, the vast grounds of Theresienwiese are transformed with beer tents run by traditional breweries, fairground rides and vendors selling gingerbread hearts and fresh pretzels. Whether they opt for traditional costume or not, visitors and locals alike love to indulge in this biggest of Bavarian bashes.

① O'Zapft Is!
At noon on the first Saturday of Oktoberfest, Munich's mayor taps the first beer barrel in the Schottenhamel tent and declares to the crowds "O'zapft is!" (it's tapped!) as the beer starts to flow.

② Bavaria Statue
In 1843, Ludwig I commissioned Leo von Klenze to build the Rohmeshalle (Hall of Fame) on the Theresien-höhe, which houses the busts of famous Bavarians. The colossal statue embodying Bavaria rises up in front. A platform inside its head offers a spectacular view of the Wiesn area.

⑤ Hearts
Every year, old and new messages appear on these traditional gingerbread hearts (left) on sale at the Wiesn. They make perfect souvenirs, along with the 1-litre Maß beer glass.

③ Memorial
On 26 September 1980, a bomb exploded at the Wiesn, killing 13 people and injuring over 200 more. A stele stands here as a reminder of this neo-Nazi attack.

④ Weißbier Carousel
One of the quirkier of the Oktoberfest drinking spots, this is the largest mobile bar on a carousel (right) in the world – for adults only.

9 Arrival of the Wiesn-Wirte

The arrival of the landlords' (on Saturday) is the prelude to the opening of the Wiesn. Their carriages **(left)** are drawn by brightly decorated show horses from the brewery.

10 Rides

With traditional fairground attractions such as the merry-go-round and Ferris wheel, and thrill rides, such as Skyfall and Olympia **(below)**, there's something for everyone, from kids to adults.

8 Beer Tents

In the large beer tents like the Pschorr-Bräurosl **(left)**, alcohol is king. Patrons link arms and sway to the music of brass bands, and challenge each other to drink another Maß of beer.

6 Beim Schichtl

Welcome to the cabaret – this theatre has been a Wiesn fixture since 1871. You can still watch traditional performances today, such as the "beheading" of an audience member by the guillotine.

7 Flea Circus

Another old-time Oktoberfest tradition not to be missed – these tiny trained creatures and their masters have been entertaining spectators on the Wiesn every year since 1948.

NEED TO KNOW

MAP JK4–5 ▪ U4/5: Theresienwiese, U3/6: Goetheplatz or Poccistraße ▪ Mid-Sep–early Oct ▪ www.oktoberfest.de

Beer Tents: open 10am–11:30pm Mon–Fri (from 9am Sat & Sun); Käfer's Wiesenschänke until 1am

Rides: open 10am–11:30pm Mon–Thu (until midnight Fri & Sat)

▪ Oktoberfest has its own service centre with a police station, health centre, lost property, a lost child point, luggage storage, an ATM and even a post office.

▪ The Oide Wiesn, a nostalgic Old Oktoberfest in period costume, with traditional marquees and stalls, is held every two years at the southern end of the Theresienwiese.

▪ On family day *(noon–6pm Tue)* rides and performances cost less.

▪ The kiosks *(open 10am–11:30pm Mon–Thu, 10am–midnight Fri & Sat)* are a great place to buy souvenirs.

🔟 ⭐ Neuschwanstein

An idealized vision of a knight's castle on the outside and a homage to Wagner's operas on the inside, Neuschwanstein was Ludwig II's most ambitious project. During the same period, he also commissioned two French-style castles: Linderhof and Herrenchiemsee. Around 1.5 million visitors each year visit Neuschwanstein, and it is consequently busy all year round. But don't let this put you off – a day trip from Munich out to Füssen is unmissable.

Throne Hall ①
Gold, saints and a touch of Byzantium: the throne hall **(right)** is modelled in part after Munich's Allerheiligen-Hofkirche and the Hagia Sophia in Istanbul. This ceremonial hall extends over the third and fourth floors – the throne was originally supposed to stand like an altar in the apse.

② Bedroom
In contrast to the romanticism of the rest of the living quarters, the bedroom is made in Gothic style complete with elaborately carved oak panelling. Scenes from Wagner's *Tristan and Isolde* decorate the walls.

③ Grotto
Moving between the living room and study, visitors pass through a small grotto **(left)**, where a waterfall flowed during the king's lifetime. The larger Venus grotto, complete with an artificial lake, is located in the park of Linderhof Palace *(see p134)*.

④ Dining Room
Dishes were transported in a lift from the kitchen three storeys below to the dining room, where the reclusive king took most of his meals, usually on his own. The murals in this predominantly red room depict the tradition of the minstrel's song.

9 The Building
The foundation stone was laid in 1869, the gatehouse completed in 1873, and the palace **(left)** finished in 1884. Work continued, with the king constantly altering plans, until his death. The keep and knight's bath were never finished.

5 Winter Garden
Adjoining the grotto, the winter garden affords a spectacular view of the Allgäu region through its large windows.

6 Hohen-schwangau
Ludwig spent part of his childhood and youth in this summer palace **(below)**, which is set in wildly romantic scenery.

7 Minstrel's Room
The castle's largest room **(below)** was based on the ceremonial hall of the Wartburg castle in Eisenach. The walls are adorned with the Legend of Percival.

8 Chapel
The chapel's altar and murals depict Louis IX, the beatified monarch of France and namesake of Ludwig II, king of Bavaria.

10 Study
Ludwig's study is filled with murals from Wagner's opera *Tannhäuser*. On his desk is a fanciful writing set in the shape of *Lohengrin*.

NEED TO KNOW

Schwangau bei Füssen ▪ (083) 6293 0830 ▪ www. neuschwanstein.de

Open Apr–mid-Oct: 9am–6pm daily; mid-Oct–Mar: 10am–4pm daily (ticket centre: open Apr–mid-Oct: 7:30am–5pm daily; mid-Oct–Mar: 8:30am–3pm daily); closed 1 Jan, Shrove Tue, 24, 25 & 31 Dec

Adm €15; concessions €14; including Hohenschwan-gau: €31, concessions €25; under-18s free

▪ Tickets (with an exact start time) are only available from the Hohenschwangau ticket centre, located below the palace. Expect to queue for tickets dur-ing peak season.

▪ Thirty-minute guided tours are the only way to visit the palace. Tours for wheelchair users are available if booked in advance. Family tours are also available, but only during school holidays, at weekends and on public holidays.

▪ The walk from the ticket centre to the castle takes 30–40 minutes; horse-drawn carriages and a shuttle bus are available.

▪ The former Grandhotel Alpenrose in Hohen-schwangau is now home to the Museum der bayerischen Könige or the Museum of Bavarian Kings *(Alpseestraße 28; (083) 62 9264640)*.

The Top 10 of Everything

**The façade of Museum Brandhorst:
36,000 ceramic rods in 23 colours**

Moments in History

① 1158: Foundation of the City

Henry the Lion, Duke of Bavaria, tore down the old salt bridge in 1157–8 and erected a new crossing over the Isar river just a few kilometres further south. There, the small market town of Munichen developed into the royal city of Munich. The day on which the Hohenstaufen Emperor Friedrich Barbarossa awarded the town the right to hold a market and mint coins (14 June 1158) is still celebrated as Munich's birthday.

Ludwig the Bavarian (1967) by Hans Wimmer

Henry the Lion, Duke of Bavaria

② 1240–1918: The Wittelsbach Dynasty

The Wittelsbachs are one of the oldest noble families in Germany. Following the deposition of Henry the Lion, the Duchy of Bavaria was passed on to Otto I in 1180. From 1240 onwards, the Wittelsbach dynasty was instrumental in defining the evolution of the city. They graduated from simple dukes to electors and finally to kings. Ludwig I commissioned classical public buildings in Munich, whereas Ludwig II built enormous, fairy tale palaces. The last ruler of the Wittelsbach dynasty, Ludwig III, fled Bavaria after World War I.

③ 1328: Ludwig the Bavarian – Holy Roman Emperor

In 1314, Duke Ludwig IV ("the Bavarian") was elected king of Germany. In 1328, he was crowned emperor of the Holy Roman Empire.

④ 1442: Expulsion of the Jews from Munich

Following pogroms against the Jews in the 13th and 14th centuries, Duke Albrecht III gave the order to expel all Jews from Upper Bavaria in 1442.

⑤ 1806: Capital of the Kingdom of Bavaria

In the wake of the Napoleonic redrafting of Europe, the electorate of Bavaria was elevated to a kingdom, with Munich as its capital and royal residence. The boundaries of Bavaria at that time were roughly the same as they are today.

⑥ 1848: March Revolution – Abdication of Ludwig I

In 1848, revolutionary uprisings reached Munich, culminating in the storming of the Zeughaus (armoury, now the Stadtmuseum). Having lost the confidence of the court and the bourgeoisie, Ludwig I was forced to abdicate.

⑦ 1918–19: November Revolution and Räterepublik

On 8 November 1918, socialist Kurt Eisner proclaimed the "Free State of Bavaria" in the Mathäserbräu building and became president for a brief period. Following his assassination on 21 February 1919, *Räterepubliken*

(Soviet republics) emerged in Munich and other cities, but were quickly suppressed by the government.

After the Assassination, Bachrach-Bareé

8 1935–45: "Capital of the Movement"

Hitler's party, the NSDAP, grew out of a small nucleus that began in Munich. As early as 1923, Hitler attempted his first coup ("Hitlerputsch") against the Weimar Republic. Munich was given the title "Capital of the Movement" in 1935, after the Nazis seized power.

9 1962: Schwabing Riots

In the summer of 1962, harmless buskers were a catalyst for violent clashes between youths and the Munich police forces that lasted for several days. These events inspired the city to rethink its hard-line policy on police intervention.

10 1972: Olympic Games

Munich hosted the Olympic Games in 1972, but the event was overshadowed by a terrorist attack against the team from Israel. In 2022, the city marked the 50th anniversary of the games with a series of sporting events and music concerts.

Munich's Olympic Stadium

TOP 10 FAMOUS CITIZENS

1 Asam brothers
Cosmas Damian (1687–1739) and Egid Quirin (1692–1750) Asam were the chief proponents of the Bavarian Rococo art movement.

Egid Quirin Asam

2 Maximilian Joseph von Montgelas
The aristocratic Montgelas (1759–1838) is the politician widely acknowledged as the creator of the modern Bavarian state.

3 Ludwig I
Numerous magnificent buildings were built by King Ludwig I (1786–1868). In 1826, he transferred the university from Landshut to Munich.

4 Lola Montez
As the mistress of Ludwig I, Lola Montez (1818–61) is said to have had great influence on the sovereign.

5 Ludwig II
"Kini" Ludwig II (1845–86) has gone down in history as the "fairy tale king". His death in the Starnberger See lake remains a mystery to this day.

6 Franz von Lenbach
The "Painter Prince" (1836–1904) was renowned for his portraits and had a huge influence on Munich's art scene.

7 Franz von Stuck
Stuck (1863–1928) was a co-founder of the Munich Secession. His Art Nouveau villa is now a museum *(see p111)*.

8 Thomas Mann
Nobel Laureate in Literature, Mann (1875–1955) spent some of his younger life in Munich.

9 Empress Elisabeth "Sisi"
Born and brought up in the city, the Wittelsbach duchess married Austrian Emperor Franz Joseph in 1854. Known as "Sisi", she was possibly the best-known woman in Europe at the time.

10 Scholl Siblings
Hans (1918–43) and Sophie (1921–43) Scholl were active in the "White Rose" resistance group in the early years of World War II. They were denounced in 1943 and executed.

🔟 Places of Worship

Choir figures by Erasmus Grasser, Frauenkirche

1 Frauenkirche

Munich's 15th-century cathedral (see pp14–15) dominates the city's skyline with its twin towers.

2 Asamkirche

Officially known as the Church of St John of Nepomuk (see p81), this late Baroque structure was designed, financed and built in the 18th century by the Asam brothers. It is located between two houses, one of which belonged to the Asams, and features opulent ceiling frescoes depicting the eponymous saint.

3 Ludwigskirche

Friedrich von Gärtner built this church (1829–43), which is flanked by two towers in Italian Romanesque style. The *Judgment Day* fresco by Peter von Cornelius displayed inside is the second-largest church fresco (see p103) in the world and definitely worth a visit.

4 Michaelskirche

MAP M3 ▪ Neuhauser Straße 6 ▪ Open 7:30am–7pm Mon–Sat, 10am–10pm Sun ▪ www.st-michael-muenchen.de

St Michael's Church today lies right in the heart of the pedestrian zone. Built for the Jesuits and completed in 1597, it is the largest late Renaissance church north of the Alps, having the second-largest barrel vault in the world after St Peter's in Rome. Its crypt contains the sarcophagi of Elector Maximilian I and Ludwig II. Look out for the bronze figure of St Michael battling the dragon, dating from 1585, on the east façade.

5 Peterskirche

The oldest parish church (see pp78–9) in the city (dating from the 13th century) is affectionately known as "Alter Peter" (Old Pete). Its interior is an eclectic mix of Gothic, Baroque and Rococo styles. Brave the 302 steps to the top of the Renaissance tower for superlative views over the old town.

The ornate ceiling of Peterskirche

6 Theatinerkirche

The Theatinerkirche *(see p91)* on Odeonsplatz stands out from the crowd with its ochre façade and pure white interior. Construction of this church, which is also called St Cajetan, began in 1663 to mark the birth of the heir to Elector Ferdinand. It is the most Italianate of all the churches in Munich.

Façade detail, Klosterkirche St Anna

7 Klosterkirche and Pfarrkirche St Anna

MAP P3 ▪ Klosterkirche: St-Anna-Straße 19; open 6am–7pm; Pfarrkirche St Anna: Sankt-Anna-Platz 5; open 8am–6pm daily ▪ www.erzbistum-muenchen.de/StAnnaMuenchen

The Lehel district is home to Munich's earliest Rococo church, built by Johann Michael Fischer in 1727–33. The church's interior design can be attributed mainly to the Asam brothers. The nearby Neo-Romanesque parish church of St Anna was constructed much later, in 1887–92.

8 Synagoge Ohel Jakob

Munich's main synagogue *(see p80)*, Ohel Jakob ("Jacob's tent") in Sankt-Jakobs-Platz, forms part of the city's Jewish centre, together with its Jewish Museum and the Israelite Community of Munich. Dating from 2006, this cube-shaped building is crowned with a glass structure and a bronze metallic grid that allows light to flood in. Its sturdy construction, with its irregular, unpolished stonework, is reminiscent of the Western Wall in Jerusalem. Visits are by prearranged tour only.

9 Damenstiftskirche St Anna

MAP M3–4
▪ Damenstiftstraße 1
▪ Open 8am–8pm daily

Originally a convent for the Sisters of the Salesian Order in the Hacken quarter of Munich's old town, St Anna's church is now a school. The late Baroque building dates from 1735, and both the façade and the interior were designed by the Asam brothers. After the church's destruction in World War II, its frescoes were recreated in sepia.

10 Heiliggeistkirche

MAP N4 ▪ Tal 77 ▪ Open 9am–8pm daily ▪ www.heilig-geist-muenchen.de

This church on Viktualienmarkt is one of the oldest in Munich. The 13th century saw the construction of a hospital church on this site, followed by a Gothic basilica in 1392. In 1724, it was remodelled in Baroque style. The interior blends Gothic and late Baroque. The stucco work is by the Asam brothers.

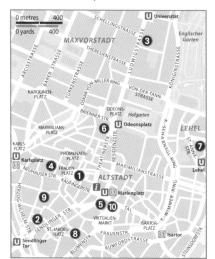

🔟 Museums and Galleries

Pinakothek der Moderne, designed by architect Stephan Braunfels

1 Pinakotheken

Known as the Pinakotheken, the Alte *(see pp18–19)* and Neue Pinakothek and the Pinakothek der Moderne *(see p20)* house the city's major art collections. The nearby Museum Brandhorst *(see p21)* is also worth a visit.

2 Deutsches Museum

There's fun for the young and old at this science and engineering museum *(see pp26–9)*.

3 Bayerisches National-museum

With its variety of cultural and histor-ical collections, the national museum *(see p105)* is one of the largest of its kind in Europe. Its exhibits include Gothic sculptures, wall hangings and clocks. The folklore section has a collection of cribs.

Byzantine art, Bayerisches Nationalmuseum

4 Münchner Stadtmuseum

This museum *(see p80)* occupies Munich's former armoury and stables, along with various other buildings. Documenting the history and culture of the city, its permanent exhibits include sections on puppetry/showmanship, photography and National Socialism in Munich. It is also home to the Film Museum *(see p56)* where many silent films have been pieced back together.

5 Glyptothek and Staatliche Antikensammlungen

The exquisite collection of Greek and Roman sculptures and bas-reliefs at the Glyptothek *(see p97)* includes 2,500-year-old gable sculp-tures from the temple of Aphaea, whose orig-inal colouring has been restored. The Antikensammlungen *(see p97)* has antique jewellery, bronzes and Greek ceramics on display.

6 Städtische Galerie im Lenbachhaus

Lenbachhaus – once the villa and studio of master painter Franz von Lenbach – contains the famous col-lection of works from the Blue Rider group *(see p97)*. The expanded, reno-vated complex also holds a large collection of 19th-century German art, while its 20th-century works include artist's rooms, photography, and installations and sculptures by Joseph Beuys.

7 Jüdisches Museum München

This museum (see p80) reflects the breadth of Jewish history, art and culture in Munich, and hosts a series of special exhibits.

8 Museum Villa Stuck

Preserved in its original Art Nouveau style, the villa (see p111) of Secessionist Franz von Stuck (1863–1928) houses a permanent exhibition in the living rooms, with paintings by the master himself, as well as special exhibitions in the adjoining studio.

9 Haus der Kunst

Today, Adolf Hitler's monument to propaganda (1932–7) is used as a venue (see p104) for international art exhibitions.

10 BMW Museum

Considered one of the best car museums in Germany, BMW has a great collection of classic vintage vehicles. Housed in a giant metallic bowl, this brilliant museum (see p128) features architecture as bold as the cars and motorbikes inside. Vehicles ranging from the earliest models to the boxy cars of the 1980s are on display.

The BMW museum near BMW Welt

TOP 10 OTHER MUSEUMS AND GALLERIES

Exhibits at Sammlung Schack

1 Sammlung Schack
This collection (see p105) showcases 19th-century masterpieces from the German art world, including works by Von Böcklin, Spitzweg and Schwind.

2 Staatliches Museum Ägyptischer Kunst
Art from Egypt is the main attraction at this museum (see p98).

3 Deutsches Theatermuseum
Located in the Hofgarten arcades, this museum (see p92) covers the history of German theatre.

4 Paläontologisches Museum
Archaeopteryx bavarica, a prehistoric bird, is a highlight at this dinosaur museum (see p100).

5 Valentin Karlstadt Musäum
Curios relating to Karl Valentin and his sidekick, Liesl Karlstadt, can be found in this museum (see p82).

6 Archäologische Staatssammlung
This museum (see p106) has prehistoric, Roman and medieval exhibits.

7 Alpines Museum
A museum (see p112) dedicated to the mountains, with a garden exhibit.

8 Museum Fünf Kontinente
This museum (see p112) has hosted global cultural exhibits since 1926 – from the oldest kayak in North America to a replica Shiva temple.

9 Kunsthalle der Hypo-Kulturstiftung
Outstanding contemporary art exhibitions are on display at this museum (see p91).

10 Lothringer 13
MAP Q5 ▪ Lothringer Straße 13
Modern multimedia is on display in this converted factory.

TOP 10 Parks and Gardens

Visitors enjoying the sun at the Englischer Garten

1 Englischer Garten

The Englischer Garten *(see pp22–3)* is a recreational paradise in the city. Every summer, thousands flock to lounge on its lawns, ride bikes and jog or skate around the many pathways, while the Kleinhesseloher lake brims with boats. For a spot of refreshment, enjoy a cold brew in one of the park's four beer gardens.

2 Alter Botanischer Garten

MAP L3 ■ Sophienstraße 7

The former Botanischer Garten was once located in this small

The Alter Botanischer Garten

park, which was also home to the 1854 Glaspalast before it burned down in 1931. Conveniently located near the pedestrian zone between Stachus and the Hauptbahnhof, it now serves as the perfect oasis for relaxing after a shopping spree.

3 Schlosspark Nymphenburg

Enclosed by a wall, this 2-km (1-mile) wide park *(see pp30–31)* stretches to the west from the Nymphenburg palace. Various picturesque pavilions and follies are scattered throughout the park, which has been declared a nature reserve to protect its 300-year-old trees.

4 Westpark

Westpark *(see p121)* was created in 1983 for the International Horticultural Exposition. An area of 72 ha (178 acres) was landscaped with numerous artificial hills, pathways, a lake and ponds. The lakeside stage hosts concerts and plays and screens films in summer.

5 Botanischer Garten

Created in Schlosspark Nymphenburg in 1914, this *(see p129)* is one of the most important otanical gardens in the world. Some 4,000 plant species from around he globe are cultivated here.

6 Bavariapark

This small park *(see p119)*, which lies directly behind the *Bavaria* statue, was established between 826 and 1831. Today, it is a great spot to take a break from the hustle and bustle of Oktoberfest.

7 Hofgarten

The Hofgarten on the north side of the Residenz was created in the style of Italian Renaissance gardens. Bounded on two sides by long arcades, it has rows of linden, chestnut and maple trees that provide welcome shade for boules players in the summer. On balmy summer evenings, tango aficionados meet up for dancing at the Temple

of Diana, a 12-sided pavilion that is topped with a shallow dome, and located in the centre of the park.

8 Luitpoldpark

Created in celebration of Prince Regent Luitpold's 90th birthday in 1911, this park *(see p106)* was extended in 1950 to include the Luitpoldhügel, a hill built out of rubble. From here there's a fine view of the city – on clear days, you can see all the way to the Alps.

9 Hirschgarten

The wild deer enclosure in this garden *(see p128)* is a reminder of its former function as a hunting park for the nobility. The park is now popular among lovers of recreational sports and its beer garden is said to be the largest in the world.

10 Isarauen and Rosengarten

MAP E6 ■ Open summer: 8am–8pm daily; winter: 9am–4pm daily

A long stretch of the Isarauen river meadows forms another of Munich's welcome green spaces. South of the Wittelsbach Bridge is the rose garden – an oasis of tranquillity in the busy city. The small complex also includes an aromatic garden, a garden with poisonous plants and a touch garden for the visually impaired.

he Temple of Diana in the Hofgarten

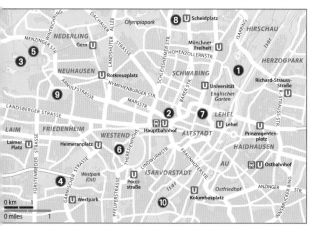

 Sport and Wellness

Bouldering at the Boulderwelt München West

1 Bouldering
www.boulderwelt.de

Bouldering is a form of rock climbing performed without the use of ropes or harnesses. Munich has two large bouldering halls – Boulderwelt München Ost (Ostbahnhof) and München West (Neuaubing).

2 Curling

Bavarian curling – also known as ice stock sport – has a long tradition in Munich. It involves competitors sliding ice stocks over an ice surface and is frequently played in the city's beer gardens during winter.

ALLIANZ ARENA

The Allianz Arena in Fröttmaning, northern Munich, was built for the World Cup in 2006 and is used by the city's two professional football clubs. Designed by architects Herzog & de Meuron, it has a transparent façade that can be illuminated in numerous colours. Holding 66,000 spectators, the stadium includes an enormous food court. The stadium can be reached via U-Bahn line U6.

Allianz Arena

---

3 Rock Climbing
www.kbthalkirchen.de

Munich is an ideal spot for fans of climbing; after all, the Alps are practically on its doorstep. The city is home to a number of artificial climbing walls for practising on before heading into the great outdoors to try out a real rock face.

4 Jogging
www.mrrc.de

Munich has plentiful parks of all sizes that are perfect for jogging (see pp46–7). The most beautiful paths are to be found in the Englischer Garten and along the banks of the Isar. If you prefer not to jog on your own, contact the local organization Roadrunners, which can put you in touch with a group of runners at your level.

5 Hiking
www.alpenverein.de

There are plenty of beautiful hiking trails in and around Munich that make for easy walking. If you prefer a more extreme challenge, take a trip to the nearby Alps for mountain hiking. For information on the best routes, contact an organization like the Deutscher Alpenverein.

6 Golf
www.muenchen-spielt-golf.de

Golf is popular in Munich and the surrounding area, so much so that golfers can choose from more than 40 golf courses dotted in and around the Bavarian capital.

⑦ Cycling
www.adfc-bayern.de

Home to one of the best cycling path networks in Europe, Munich has several green routes that you can follow without the nuisance of exhaust fumes and noise. Check with the ADFC (German Cyclist's Association) for a variety of cycling tours in and around Munich.

⑧ Watersports
SWM: www.swm.de/english/m-baeder/indoor-pools

Munich and the nearby lake regions are a haven in summer for anyone who enjoys swimming, rowing, sailing, windsurfing or canoeing. Destinations range from city swimming pools (maintained by SWM) to quarry ponds, small, idyllic moor lakes and the great lakes of Upper Bavaria.

Wellness treatment at Sai Spa

⑨ Wellness
www.sai-spa.de

Munich has responded to the rising popularity of wellness and offers a wide range of facilities, from the day spa at the organic supermarket to the Blue Spa in Bayerischer Hof. The Turkish bath at the Mathildenbad is hugely popular, while for an Asian-style ambience, Sai Spa is another good choice.

⑩ Winter Sports
www.winter-muenchen.de

The city and its environs are a hub for winter sports fans, whether you like skiing, ice skating, snowboarding, curling or sledging. With such a wide variety of winter sports, there's something for everyone.

TOP 10 EVENTS AND TEAMS

Munich marathon

1 Vierschanzen-Tournee
New Year ▪ www.vierschanzen tournee.com
The best-known ski jump tournament in the world, held in Oberstdorf, Garmisch-Partenkirchen, Innsbruck and Bischofshofen.

2 BMW Open
Apr/May ▪ www.bmwopen.de
This tennis tournament is held at the MTTC Iphitos club.

3 BMW International Open
Jun ▪ www.bmw-golfsport.com
The annual golf tournament often takes place around Munich.

4 Munich Mash
Late Jun ▪ www.munich-mash.com
See the pros in action performing stunts at Olympiapark.

5 Isarschwimmen
First day of Oktoberfest
▪ www.isarschwimmen.de
This traditional swimming event sees brave individuals take to the Isar canal.

6 Munich Marathon
Oct ▪ www.generalimuenchen marathon.de
An annual race through the city.

7 Winter Running
Dec–Feb ▪ www.olympiapark.de
A series of races in Olympiapark on three courses (10, 15 & 20 km).

8 Harness Racing
All year ▪ www.daglfing.de
Held at the Munich Daglfing racecourse.

9 FC Bayern Munich
www.fcbayern.de
Germany's world-famous football club has been picking up titles for decades.

10 TSV 1860 Munich
www.tsv1860.de
Fans of the city's second football club refer to the team as "the Lions".

Off the Beaten Track

The Bayerische Volkssternwarte

1 Bayerische Volks-sternwarte München

MAP H6 ■ Rosenheimer Straße 45h
■ Tours: Apr–Aug: 9pm Mon–Fri,
Sep–Mar: 8pm Mon–Fri ■ Adm
■ www.sternwarte-muenchen.de

This public observatory was
established by a group of amateur
astronomers after World War II.
In addition to the telescopes on the
observation platform, it also has a
planetarium and hosts exhibitions
and lectures by astronomers. There
are also tours aimed at children.

2 Designer U-Bahn Stations

Munich's U-Bahn stations really pack
a punch: the Marienplatz mezzanine
is painted a rich orange-red; lighting
designer Ingo Maurer had some
great fun with blue at Münchner
Freiheit; and Westfriedhof is awash
with red, yellow and blue. Georg-
Brauchle-Ring features a whole host
of different colours, while Candidplatz
is embellished with rainbow effects.
In 2014, Munich's U-Bahn trains won
the German Design Award.

3 Der Verrückte Eismacher

MAP N1 ■ Amalienstraße 77
■ Open daily

With ice cream flavours ranging from
the fairly traditional, such as nutty-
chocolate, melon or kiwi lime, to the
more unusual – cheese-and-chive,
beer or asparagus, for example –
this popular parlour offers a long
list of extraordinary concoctions
that changes on a daily basis.

4 Summer Tango

MAP N2 & P4 ■ Hofgarten
and Praterinsel

The unofficial meeting point of
Munich's tango fans is the Temple of
Diana in the Hofgarten *(see p17)*. The
otherwise strict site management
allows dancers to take part in salsa
(Wed and Sun), swing dance (Sun
afternoon) and tango (Fri) sessions.
Another of these meeting points can
be found in the inner courtyard of the
former distillery on the Praterinsel.

Rainbow shades at Candidplatz U-Bahn station

⑤ Löwenturm am Rindermarkt
MAP N4 ■ Rindermarkt 9

The origins of this 12th-century, 23-m (75-ft) high tower are a bit of a mystery. It was presumably part of the town ramparts, but could have also been a water tower. Unfortunately, it isn't possible to access the interior to see its ribbed vaults and frescos.

⑥ Hofgarten Boules
MAP N2 ■ Hofgarten (north side)

The Hofgarten has been a popular meeting point for boules players for over 40 years. When the weather is good, they flock to the park to play, lending it a Mediterranean atmosphere. There's a boules tournament held here every July, but you can watch players enjoying a game throughout the summer months.

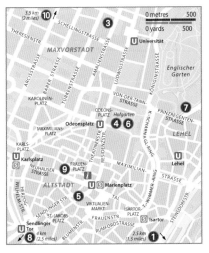

Boules players at the Hofgarten

⑦ Fräulein Grüneis
MAP P2 ■ Lerchenfeldstraße 1a ■ Open daily until dusk

On the banks of the Eisbach in the Englischer Garten, not far from where the surfers hang out, there was once a little toilet block. It was then transformed into a pleasant café kiosk serving exclusively organic goodies, including coffee, sandwiches and cakes. Hot lunch dishes are served daily.

⑧ Gans am Wasser
MAP C6 ■ Mollsee in Westpark ■ Opening hours vary, check website for details ■ www.gansamwasser.de

This rustic café is a popular meeting place for locals all year round. Delicious food, such as kebabs and bratwürst rolls, is served alongside a variety of cocktails and beers. The café is located on the banks of the Mollsee river and also hosts music events and yoga sessions.

⑨ Bronze Model of the City
MAP M3 ■ Frauenplatz

The Frauenkirche serves as the backdrop for this bronze model of Munich's old town, created by Egbert Broerken in 2005. Not only does it help those with visual impairments to find their bearings, but it provides a wonderfully tactile and visual experience for all.

⑩ Olympia-Alm
MAP E1 ■ Martin-Luther-King-Weg 8 ■ Open noon–midnight daily

The highest beer garden in Munich perches on top of the Olympiaberg at 564 m (1,850 ft). Originally just a kiosk to serve the workers constructing the Olympic Park in 1972, it now offers beer and a selection of hearty Bavarian fare, including Glühwein in winter.

Children's Attractions

Olympiapark

Kids who enjoy sport will love the range of activities on offer at the Olympic Park (see pp32–3). Whether it's the aquatic centre, beach volleyball court, ski slope, boat centre, streetball court or – for older kids – climbing tours on the tent roof, the jam-packed programme at Olympiapark is the best in the city.

2 Tierpark Hellabrunn

Highlights of the city zoo (see pp120–21) include talks about elephants, polar bears, and Siberian tigers. For younger kids, there's also a petting zoo, play areas and "Kinderland". Be sure to experience one of the animal walks, where you can get up close to the llamas or ponies.

3 Kindermuseum München

MAP L3 ▪ Arnulfstraße 3 ▪ (089) 5404 6440 ▪ Open 2–5pm Tue–Fri, 10am–5pm Sat, Sun & public/school hols ▪ Adm ▪ www.kindermuseum-muenchen.de

This children's museum offers interactive exhibits, workshops and plenty of games to keep the little ones occupied.

Blowing bubbles, Kindermuseum

4 Deutsches Museum

Older children will be fascinated by many of the displays at this museum (see pp26–9). There's also a kids' zone for the younger ones (ages three and up). The interactive

Hands-on exhibit, Deutsches Museum

exhibits allow children to experience physics first hand. They're sure to enjoy both the Technisches Spielzeug (Technical Toys) section and the planet walk from the sun to Pluto, which takes around an hour.

5 Marionettentheater

MAP M4 ▪ Blumenstraße 32 ▪ (089) 265712 ▪ Adm ▪ www.muema-theater.de

Munich's oldest puppet theatre, founded in 1858, is housed in a small gabled and colonnaded temple dating back to 1900. Performances are enthusiastically received by young and old alike, and the shows here can include anything from children's mysteries to *The Magic Flute*.

6 Bavaria Filmstadt

Film and television productions are still made at these studios (see p56), which offer a wide variety of guided tours. Expect explosions and excitement at the stunt show, and be sure to check out the special effects studio to find out how the seemingly impossible makes it onto the big screen. At Bullyversum, German film director and actor Michael "Bully" Herbig welcomes every visitor (almost) personally. The 4D experience cinema (children taller than 1.2 m/4 ft only) should not be missed.

7 BMW Welt

A surefire hit with a younger car-obsessed audience, BMW's mega showroom (see p129) lets you get behind the wheel of high-powered models, find out how a petrol engine works and watch motorbike riders perform stunts on the steps and floor space. There's also a café and a shop.

8 Sea Life

MAP E1 ■ Willi-Daume-Platz 1 ■ (089) 450000 ■ Open 10am–7pm daily ■ Adm ■ www.visitsealife.com

Many of the creatures at this aquarium (see p33) within the Olympiapark are on the Red List of Threatened Species. The seahorses and touch pool are firm favourites with kids, while everyone enjoys feeding time.

Deer in Wildpark Poing

9 Wildpark Poing

Osterfeldweg 20, Poing ■ (081) 218 0617 ■ Open Apr–Oct: 9am–5pm daily (Nov–Mar: until 4pm) ■ www.wildpark-poing.net

A circular route guides visitors on a journey of discovery featuring native species, enclosures and aviaries in a simulated natural habitat. There's the opportunity to feed some of the animals, and birds of prey shows take place in summer.

10 Schauburg

Housed in a former cinema, this theatre (see p54) for children puts on around 350 performances a year, all in German.

TOP 10 CHILD-FRIENDLY CAFÉS AND RESTAURANTS

Café Zuckertag

1 Café Zuckertag
MAP L6 ■ Ehrengutstraße 10
Enjoy breakfast, lunch or cake while the little ones have fun in the playroom.

2 Seehaus
Seehaus (see p23) on the Kleinhesseloher See has boats for hire.

3 Café de Bambini
MAP G2 ■ Marktstraße 7
Enjoy a coffee while clothes shopping for the kids. Little ones can play in the fun zone or tuck into baby food.

4 Chinesischer Turm
A nostalgic carousel can be found right next to the beer garden (see p23).

5 Aumeister
Sondermeierstraße 1
This beer garden in the northern part of the Englischer Garten has its own adventure playground.

6 Turncafé
MAP E3 ■ Hiltenspergerstraße 43
A play area and activity room are available for tiny tots.

7 Kaiser Otto
MAP M5 ■ Westermühlstraße 8
There are babysitters in the Kids Lounge during brunch (10am–2pm Sat & Sun).

8 Hofbräukeller
MAP Q4 ■ Innere Wiener Straße 19
This large play area offers supervision for children aged 8 and under (noon–8pm Mon–Fri, 10am–8pm Sat & Sun).

9 Vits
MAP N4 ■ Rumfordstraße 49
This popular coffee roasting house has a cosy family corner.

10 Hirschau
MAP H2 ■ Gyßlingstraße 15
The beer garden here has a perfect view of the fenced play park.

🔟 Theatre, Concerts and Opera

The Philharmonic Hall at Gasteig

1 Isarphilharmonie

The concert hall in the Gasteig HP8 cultural centre, which opened in 2021, offers space for around 1,900 visitors. The entire complex will serve as the alternative quarters for the Isar Philharmonic until the renovation of the Gasteig *(see p112)* is complete.

2 Residenztheater

In 1951, the Neues Residenztheater *(see p89)* opened its doors next to the opera house. Known as the "Resi", this theatre puts on a wide range of productions across its venues, which include the Cuvilliés-Theater and Marstall.

Performance at the Residenztheater

3 Bavarian State Opera

Run by artistic director Nikolaus Bachler and general musical director Kirill Petrenko, the opera house *(see p89)* at the national theatre draws in half a million visitors every year to over 400 performances.

4 Herkulessaal

MAP N3 ■ Residenzstraße 1 (Hofgarten entrance) ■ (089) 290671

This vast hall within the Residenz hosts a diverse range of concerts, from orchestral pieces to chamber music performances.

5 Prinzregententheater

MAP R3 ■ Prinzregentenplatz 12 ■ (089) 2185 1970 ■ www.theater akademie.de

Built in 1901 as a Wagner festival theatre, the space – conceived as an amphitheatre – is chiefly used as a performance venue for the Bayerische Theaterakademie August Everding.

6 Münchner Volkstheater

MAP E6 ■ Tumblingerstraße 29 ■ (089) 523 46 55 ■ www.muenchner-volkstheater.de

Theatregoers come here for a sophisticated repertoire of entertaining, popular plays.

⑦ Cuvilliés-Theater

Munich's most elaborate and historically significant theatre (see p17), which underwent substantial renovations around ten years ago, is used for performances by the Bayerische Staatstheater and occasionally for other musical events.

⑧ Münchner Kammerspiele

MAP N3 ▪ Maximilianstraße 28 ▪ (089) 2339 6600 ▪ www. muenchner-kammerspiele.de

Built by Richard Riemerschmid in 1901, this theatre – considered one of the best stages in Germany – became the home of the Münchner Kammerspiele. It caused a stir in the 1920s by staging the works of Bertolt Brecht.

Deutsches Theater at night

⑨ Deutsches Theater

MAP L3–4 ▪ Schwanthalerstraße 13 ▪ (089) 5523 4444 ▪ www. deutsches-theater.de

The German Theatre is the main venue for hit international musicals such as *Cats*, *Grease*, *Evita* and *West Side Story*, all translated into German, of course.

⑩ Staatstheater am Gärtnerplatz

MAP N5 ▪ Gärtnerplatz 3 ▪ www. staatstheateramgaertnerplatz.de

Built in 1865 as a bourgeois equivalent to the royal theatre houses, this intimate theatre hosts operas, operettas and musicals. It opened in late 2017 after renovation.

TOP 10 SMALL STAGES AND CABARETS

Metropoltheater, a former cinema

1 Metropoltheater
Floriansmühlstraße 5, Freimann ▪ (089) 3219 5533
This is an exceptional alternative theatre.

2 Komödie im Bayerischen Hof
MAP M3 ▪ Promenadeplatz 6 ▪ (089) 292810
Enjoy comedies and revues here.

3 HochX
MAP N6 ▪ Entenbachstraße 37 ▪ (089) 2097 0321
Art and music shows are held here.

4 TamS-Theater
MAP G2 ▪ Haimhauserstraße 13a ▪ (089) 345890
This theatre has been hosting unusual productions since 1970.

5 Teamtheater
MAP N4 ▪ Am Einlass 2a and 4 ▪ (089) 260 4333/6636
An independent theatre with two zones: "Tankstelle" & "Salon".

6 Schauburg
MAP F3 ▪ Elisabethplatz ▪ (089) 2333 7155 ▪ www.schauburg.net
A renowned stage for young people.

7 Blutenburgtheater
MAP D3 ▪ Blutenburgstraße 35 ▪ (089) 123 4300
A mystery production venue.

8 Pasinger Fabrik
August-Exter-Straße 1, München-Pasing ▪ (089) 8292 9079
Theatre and opera in the cultural centre.

9 Lach- und Schießgesellschaft
MAP G2 ▪ Ursulastraße 9 ▪ (089) 391997
This is a political cabaret with bite.

10 Theater im Fraunhofer
MAP M5 ▪ Fraunhoferstraße 9 ▪ (089) 267850
This small stage hosts everything from music to cabaret.

🔟 Bavarian Cinema

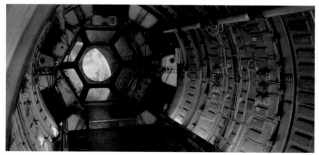

Set of the spaceship from *Stowaway* in the Bavaria Filmstadt

 ASTOR Film Lounge im ARRI Kino

MAP N1 ▪ Türkenstraße 91 ▪ (089) 3889 9664 ▪ www.arri-kino.de

Named for the ARRI movie camera company, this cinema has a large foyer area and bar.

2 Filmfest München

Since 1983, the largest German public film festival has been screening the latest international films at the end of June. The Gasteig *(see p112)* is the festival hub, with screenings held at cinemas throughout the city. The International Festival of Film Academies (Filmschool fest Munich), an offshoot of the main festival, takes place in November.

3 Bavaria Filmstadt and Bullyversum

Bavariafilmplatz 7, Geiselgasteig ▪ (089) 6499 2000 ▪ Open Mar–Oct: 9am–6pm daily; Nov–Feb: 10am–5pm daily ▪ www.filmstadt.de

Munich's suburb of Geiselgasteig has been a centre for filmmaking since 1910. Major productions have been shot here, including Wolfgang Petersen's *Das Boot* and films by Rainer Werner Fassbinder and Ingmar Bergman. Bavaria Filmstadt *(see p52)* runs a range of guided tours of the area.

4 Hochschule für Fernsehen und Film München

MAP M2 ▪ Bernd-Eichinger-Platz 1 ▪ (089) 689570 ▪ www.hff-muenchen.de

The HFF (University of Television and Film Munich) has been a training ground for filmmakers since 1967, and graduates of this prestigious institute include Wim Wenders and Roland Emmerich. The venue hosts screenings in summer.

5 Mathäser

MAP L3 ▪ Bayerstraße 3–5 ▪ (089) 515651 ▪ www.mathaeser.de

A modern multiplex cinema, which is also used for film premieres.

Poster for Filmfest München

Filmmuseum München
MAP M4 ▪ St-Jakobs-Platz 1
▪ (089) 2339 6450 (tickets) ▪ Shows
6:30 and 9pm Tue–Sun (7pm Thu)
▪ www.muenchner-stadtmuseum.de
This theatre is equipped with the latest projection technology for all film formats. For over 40 years, it has been screening foreign films, film series, films from the museum's own archives, and silent movie reconstructions (often with live music accompaniment).

DOK.fest München
May is the month of documentaries for Munich's cinemas, with three popular competitions. The festival also serves as a get-together for those in the industry.

Open-Air cinema, Olympiapark

Fantasy Filmfest
A penchant for genre cinema is a prerequisite for this festival of non-mainstream films, ranging from horror to thrillers and sci-fi (Aug/Sep).

Open-Air Cinemas
If you're looking to enjoy a film in the great outdoors during the summer, head to the open-air cinemas in Olympiapark, Westpark, Viehhof or Königsplatz.

Werkstattkino
MAP M5 ▪ Fraunhoferstraße 9 ▪ (089) 260 7250 ▪ www.werkstattkino.de
Tucked away in the basement of a rear courtyard building, this cinema is dedicated to screening films outside the mainstream, which are often shown in their original languages.

TOP 10 MUNICH FILMMAKERS

Rainer-W.-Fassbinder-Platz

1 Percy Adlon
This director (b. 1935) worked in Hollywood following the unexpected success of *Out of Rosenheim*.

2 Herbert Achternbusch
This agent provocateur (b. 1938) known for film, writing and painting, creates anarchic Bavarian films.

3 The Verhoevens
Michael Verhoeven (b. 1938) belongs to a prominent family of actors and directors, and is married to actress Senta Berger.

4 Joseph Vilsmaier
This successful director (b. 1939) is famous for his biopics, such as *Comedian Harmonists* (1997).

5 May Spils
With her 1967 *Zur Sache Schätzchen*, Spils (b. 1941) created the film that captured the spirit of Schwabing.

6 Helmut Dietl
Dietl (1944–2015) depicted Munich in TV series such as *Monaco Franze* (1983) and *Kir Royal* (1985).

7 Rainer Werner Fassbinder
Famous prodigy of the New German Cinema, Fassbinder (1945–82) directed more than 40 films.

8 Doris Dörrie
Since rising to fame with her 1985 film *Männer*, director and author Dörrie (b. 1955) has won numerous awards.

9 Caroline Link/Dominik Graf
In 2002, Link (b. 1964) won the Oscar for Best Foreign Film for *Nirgendwo in Afrika*. She lives in Munich with fellow director, Dominik Graf (b. 1952).

10 Florian Gallenberger
Gallenberger (b. 1972) won an Oscar in 2001 for his short film *Quiero ser*.

TOP10 Nightlife

Dancefloor at indie club Strom

1 Strom
MAP K6 ■ Lindwurmstraße 88
■ Open from 10pm Fri & Sat ■ www.
strom-muc.de

Indie fans are right at home in this club on Lindwurmhof, which offers a programme of DJ parties and concerts.

2 Milla Club
MAP E6 ■ Holzstraße 28
■ Opening hours vary, check website
■ www.milla-club.de

A hip venue located in a small basement in Glockenbachviertel. Expect live music up to six times a week here, with everything from rock and indie to hip-hop and jazz.

3 Paradiso Tanzbar
Located in the rooms of the once-legendary "Old Mrs Henderson" club, which welcomed the likes of Mick Jagger, David Bowie and Freddie Mercury, the Paradiso (see p84) is now making a mark of its own. A popular club in retro 1980s style, complete with a flashing dance floor and classic retro hits.

4 Muffathalle and Ampere
MAP P4 ■ Zellstraße 4
■ www.muffatwerk.de

The Muffathalle, the smaller Ampere, and the colonnaded café are open only for scheduled events such as parties, concerts, theatre, productions, dance recitals and readings. This former heating plant is one of the most beautiful venues in the city, located right behind the Müller'sches Volksbad. The beer garden is especially inviting on a sunny day.

5 Harry Klein
MAP L3 ■ Sonnenstraße 8
■ Open from 8pm Thu, 10pm Fri & Sat ■ www.harrykleinclub.de

Harry Klein is one of a number of clubs on Sonnenstraße that have popped up in the past few years. DJ sets here range from techno house to electro, and the lighting concept creates an exciting vibe.

The Harry Klein electro club

6 P1
MAP P2 ▪ Prinzregentenstraße 1 ▪ Open from 11pm Mon–Sat ▪ www.p1-club.de

P1 (named after its address) was once a well-known hangout of the FC Bayern players, with a reputation reaching far beyond Munich. The celebrities have now largely moved on and the atmosphere is a little more chilled. Great sound quality.

7 Rote Sonne
MAP M3 ▪ Maximiliansplatz 5 ▪ Open from 10pm Fri & Sat ▪ www.rote-sonne.com

Techno and electro are the genres of choice at this funky little club on Maximiliansplatz, which hosts live gigs during the week.

The atmospheric Rote Sonne

8 Pacha
MAP M3 ▪ Maximiliansplatz 5 ▪ Open from 6:30pm Thu, 11pm Fri & Sat ▪ www.pacha-muenchen.de

This club offers the full range of house music and hosts top DJs. The outdoor terrace is a treat in the summer.

9 089 Bar
MAP M3 ▪ Maximiliansplatz 5 ▪ Open from 9pm Tue–Sat ▪ www.089-bar.de

This club on Maximiliansplatz with a central bar and dance floor is open until the early hours.

10 Bahnwärter Thiel
Techno nights, concerts and outdoor raves await visitors at Bahnwärter Thiel *(see p84)*, an arts centre created using repurposed shipping containers.

TOP 10 LGBTQ+ VENUES

The elegant Deutsche Eiche

1 Deutsche Eiche
MAP N4 ▪ Reichenbachstraße 13 ▪ www.deutsche-eiche.de
This gay pub has a hotel and sauna.

2 Café Nil
MAP M5 ▪ Hans-Sachs-Straße 2 ▪ www.cafenil.com
Café Nil is one of Munich's first gay cafés.

3 Café Glück
MAP M6 ▪ Palmstraße 4 ▪ www.cafe-glueck.com
This café offers snacks, drinks and music.

4 Jenny was a friend of mine
MAP M5 ▪ Holzstraße 14 ▪ www.jennifer-parks.com
Enjoy quiz nights and parties at this bar.

5 Ochsengarten
MAP E5 ▪ Müllerstraße 47 ▪ www.ochsengarten.de
Munich's first bar for those interested in the leather subculture.

6 NY.Club
MAP L4 ▪ Sonnenstraße 25 ▪ www.nyclub.de
A gay disco, NY.Club is open on Fridays and Saturdays.

7 Edelheiss
MAP M4 ▪ Pestalozzistraße 6 ▪ www.edelheiss.de
If you have a beard, the second beer here is free on Thursdays (8–10pm).

8 Café im Sub
MAP M4 ▪ Müllerstraße 14 ▪ www.subonline.org
LGBTQ+ communication centre and café.

9 LeZ München
MAP M4 ▪ Müllerstraße 26 ▪ www.lez-muenchen.de
LGBTQ+ community centre organizing workshops, parties and meet-ups.

10 Christopher Street Day (CSD)
www.csdmuenchen.de
Pride Week (early July) involves a parade, street party and club night.

Bars and Cafés

1 Zephyr Bar
This bar (see p84), a popular hangout in the Glockebach quarter, is known for its variety of spectacular drinks. Their motto: "Drinking is a necessity – enjoy it as an art form."

2 Maria Passagne
MAP G5 ■ Steinstraße 42
■ (089) 486167

Ring the door bell to enter this hidden cocktail bar, a favourite among Munich's artsy crowd. Inside, red lighting creates an ambient atmosphere and an assortment of quirky art lines the walls. Expect creative cocktails from the bartenders and top-notch sushi on the menu.

The cosy Flushing Meadows

3 Bar Centrale
At this Italian all-day bar and lounge (see p94), take a seat towards the front (or at one of the tables outside) and enjoy the tantalizing aroma of espresso. Head further into the bar and you'll find yourself transported back to the 1960s. The cocktails and pasta are great. Bar Centrale is set over two floors, with the bar area upstairs. The basement has the former bakery, with the original oven and wall tiles.

4 Café Frischhut
While hungover revellers once flocked to this café (see p83) from as early as 5am, it now opens around 8am. It is also known as "Schmalznudel" after its popular fresh pastries and buns.

5 Flushing Meadows
The rooftop bar (see p84) at this hotel in the Glockenbach quarter offers magnificent views of the old town. If you're lucky, you can even see as far as the Alps on a clear day. The drinks menu is a mix of classic German specialities and international favourites.

6 Alvino Bar
This bar showcases Munich at its eccentric best. You can enjoy a spot of shopping at Ed Meier and then head to Alvino bar for a drink (see p94). With its sophisticated interior and alpine details, this bar is more of a daytime or early evening venue, serving coffee, bar food and cocktails.

Pastries and buns for breakfast at the Café Frischhut

(7) Schumann's

Charles Schumann has been running this legendary bar *(see p94)* for 30 years. In a city where fashionable spots come and go, this bar has always been popular with famous and not-so-famous visitors alike. It even survived the big move from Maximilianstraße to its present location on Odeonsplatz. The first-floor bar, Les Fleurs du Mal, has a 9-m (30-ft) long table where guests can discuss drinks with the bartender, and there's a gorgeous terrace looking out towards the Hofgarten.

(8) Kilians Irish Pub

Sip on some Guinness while listening to live music at this pub *(see p84)*. The beer garden has a terrace that offers splendid views of the Frauenkirche. Traditional Irish stew and barbecue burgers are on the menu here.

The pastel pink Café Lotti

(9) Café Lotti

This attractive café *(see p101)* with pretty pastel decor is located near the Pinakotheken *(see pp18–19)*. A variety of great breakfasts, savoury and sweet snacks and beverages are served here.

(10) Café Hüller

The breakfast here *(see p116)* comes highly recommended, whether you opt for something sweet, hearty or healthy. The daily menu includes soups, vegetarian dishes and desserts.

TOP 10 BARS AND CAFÉS WITH LIVE MUSIC

1 Jazzbar Vogler
MAP N4 ▪ Rumfordstraße17
▪ (089) 294662
Blues nights, jazz concerts and readings.

2 Waldwirtschaft Großhesselohe
Georg-Kalb-Straße 3, PullachGroßhesselohe ▪ (089) 7499 4030
Popular pub staging live jazz concerts.

3 Café am Beethovenplatz
Munich's oldest café *(see p123)* with live classical music and jazz.

4 Antons
St-Martin-Straße 7 ▪ (089) 6973 7245
Restaurant and bar with live music on Saturdays.

5 Night Club
MAP M3 ▪ Promenadeplatz 2–6
▪ (089) 212 0994
The cellar in the Bayerischer Hof plays host to live acts from funk to jazz.

6 Irish Folk Pub
MAP G2 ▪ Giselastraße 11
▪ (089) 342446
Serves up Irish stew, Guinness, whiskey and live Irish folk music every Thursday.

7 Hofbräuhaus
Hofbräuhaus *(see p89)* is a must-visit if you like brass band music.

8 Wirtshaus zum Isartal
Brudermühlstraße 2 ▪ (089) 772121
A rustic tavern with a stage for plays and small productions as well as live music.

9 Baal
Kreittmayrstraße 26 ▪ (089) 1870 3836
This rustic bar hosts blues, jazz, soul and funk acts.

10 Jazzclub Unterfahrt
MAP Q4 ▪ Einsteinstraße 42 ▪ (089) 448 2794
A jazz club at the Einstein Kultur centre.

Jazzclub Unterfahrt

TOP10 Bavarian Dishes

Bratwürst with Kraut

1 Wurst and Würstl

In Bavaria, *Wurst* (sausage) is eaten as part of a cold snack known as *Brotzeit* ("bread time"). A regional speciality is *Weißwurst* (boiled veal sausage), which is cooked in boiling water and peeled out of its skin before being enjoyed with sweet mustard. Typical hot sausage dishes include *Schweinswürstl* (Franconian pork sausages) served with sauerkraut or *Leberkäse* (meat loaf). *Regensburger* (boiled sausages) are the star of the show in any self-respecting Bavarian *Wurstsalat* (sausage salad).

Plain salted pretzels

2 Münchner Schnitzel

The Wittelsbachs were related to the Habsburgs, and so many of the dishes commonly found in Bavaria were originally inspired by Bohemian Austrian cuisine, for example *Knödel*

Münchner Schnitzel, a savoury treat

(dumplings), *Mehlspeisen* (pastries) and even schnitzel. The Munich twist on schnitzel includes a horseradish, sweet mustard and *Breznbrösel* (pretzel breadcrumb) coating.

3 Schweinebraten

Succulent *Schweinebraten* (roast pork) is a real Bavarian favourite. The local way to cook it involves scoring the rind before putting the joint into the oven to roast. The meat is then continuously basted with beer (ideally dark lager) while it is roasting, until the rind develops into crispy crackling. *Schweinebraten* is traditionally served with *Knödeln* and sauerkraut or coleslaw.

4 Knödel

Dumplings are a mainstay of Bavarian cooking. Originally a means of using up leftover, stale bread rolls by soaking them, *Semmelknödel* are particularly popular. A tasty alternative is the *Breznknödel*, made with stale *Laugenbrezel* (lye pretzels). Another type is *Kartoffelknödel*, made from grated potatoes with a toasted cube of white bread in the centre. Dumplings that are made exclusively from cooked potatoes are also sometimes used for making sweet pastries, such as *Zwetschgenknödel* (plum dumplings).

⑤ Kässpätzle

A type of soft egg noodle, *Spätzle* originated in the Swabia region. The cooking method involves scraping the almost runny *Spätzle* dough into boiling water. The end product is available in a variety of different versions and dishes. One dish, known as *Allgäuer Kässpätzle*, involves cheese and minced onions.

Aubergine dish

⑥ Steckerlfisch

Those who have been to Oktoberfest will be more than familiar with the smell of this fish on a stick, typically trout, char or mackerel, cooked on a charcoal grill.

⑦ Brezn and Semmeln

The *Laugenbrezn* is the region's most popular and common type of pretzel, and its appeal skyrockets during Oktoberfest. *Semmel* is the Bavarian name for a bread roll.

⑧ Obatzda

This spreadable cheese (made from Camembert, butter, quark, paprika and onion) is a beer-garden favourite.

⑨ Süßspeisen

Bavarian *Süßspeisen* (desserts) are typically hearty. Favourites include *Apfelstrudel* (apple strudel), *Hollerkücherl* (elderflower pancakes), *Dampfnudeln* (steamed dumplings) and Austrian *Kaiserschmarrn* (shredded pancakes), often served with fruit compote.

⑩ Gebäck

The Bavarian region is home to a whole host of *Gebäck* (pastries). Anyone with a sweet tooth should look out for *Zwetschgendatschi* (plum cake), *Rohrnudeln* (sweet filled rolls made from yeast dough), and the ever-popular *Auszogne* (doughnuts).

TOP 10 VEGETARIAN AND VEGAN RESTAURANTS

1 Lost Weekend
MAP N1 ▪ Schellingstraße 3
A popular bookshop café serving vegan coffee and cake.

2 Max Pett
MAP M4 ▪ Pettenkoferstraße 8
This place serves plant-based vegan dishes. Alcohol is not available here.

3 Café Ignaz
MAP F3 ▪ Georgenstraße 67
An extensive menu featuring crêpes, gnocchi and organic beer.

4 Gratitude
MAP N1 ▪ Türkenstraße 55
This organic restaurant offers vegan, gluten-free and raw dishes.

5 Bodhi
MAP J4 ▪ Ligsalzstraße 23
Vegan Bavarian-style restaurant serving *Obatzda* and schnitzel burgers.

6 Vegelangelo
MAP P4 ▪ Thomas-Wimmer-Ring 15
The vegetarian food here packs a real punch, from the pasta creations to the truffle risotto.

7 TIAN
MAP N4 ▪ Frauenstraße 4
This restaurant by Viktualienmarkt offers meat-free delights with a gourmet feel.

8 Deli Kitchen
MAP L2 ▪ Augustenstraße 5
A vegan shop with its own small stylish restaurant.

9 Tushita Teehaus
MAP M5 ▪ Klenzestraße 53
Great teas and fresh vegan snacks.

10 Prinz Myshkin
Munich's top vegetarian restaurant *(see p83)* is known for serving imaginative and flavourful meat-free and vegan dishes.

Appetizers at Prinz Myshkin

Restaurants

1 Vinaiolo

Located in the Haidhausen area, this restaurant (see p117) has a nostalgic shop-style interior and represents the perfect blend of an osteria, a bistro and a wine cellar. Guests can expect to enjoy inspired Italian cuisine along with accompanying wines (at reasonable prices). Good-value lunchtime menus and a four-course evening menu are available.

2 Tantris

The two-Michelin-starred Tantris (see p109) has long been considered one of the best restaurants in Germany. Canadian chef Benjamin Chmura has been at the helm since 2021, bringing his philosophy of indulgence to the restaurant. Guests can choose between six and eight courses for dinner, while no fewer than three sommeliers advise on the impressive wine offerings. This is the perfect venue for celebrating a special occasion – not least due to its bold, retro decor, which almost steals the show from the food.

The bright dining room at Zauberberg

3 Zauberberg

MAP D3 ▪ Hedwigstraße 14 ▪ (089) 1899 9178 ▪ Closed Sun–Tue, L ▪ www.restaurant-zauberberg.de ▪ €€€

Zauberberg is renowned for creating innovative dishes from fresh, seasonal ingredients. An early-bird three-course menu (€33) is available from 6 to 7pm on Wednesdays and Thursdays. This bright, friendly restaurant also has outdoor seating.

4 Pageou

Ali Güngörmüş, whose restaurant Le Canard Nouveau (now closed) won a Michelin star, serves modern cuisine at this restaurant (see p95) in the Fünf Höfe shopping centre. The dining area has its own gallery on a mezzanine level for smaller groups, as well as an inner courtyard terrace. The restaurant also has an extensive wine list that features around 300 varieties of wine.

5 Landersdorfer and Innerhofer

This traditional wine restaurant (see p83) has a friendly atmosphere and a menu that changes daily. Hans Landersdorfer's Austrian-inspired menu is a pure delight. Wine recommendations are provided by Robert Innerhofer, and there is a two-course lunch menu for €25.

Retro interior at Tantris

6 Matsuhisa Munich

The only restaurant (see p95) in Germany headed by top chef Nobu Matsuhisa can be found in Munich's Mandarin Oriental hotel. The fusion of Japanese and Peruvian cuisine might not come cheap, but it's definitely worth it. The yellowtail sashimi, Peruvian rib eye *anticucho* and whiskey cappuccino are the main highlights here.

7 Restaurant Alois

Head chef Christoph Kunz serves up spectacular dishes at this Michelin-starred fine-dining restaurant (see p95), located on the first floor of Munich's most illustrious delicatessen (see p93). Reserve a table months in advance to savour his gourmet creations amid dramatic interiors.

Table setting at Geisel's Vinothek

8 Geisel's Vinothek

MAP L3 ▪ Schützenstraße 11 ▪ (089) 5 5137 7140 ▪ Closed Sun L ▪ www.excelsior-hotel.de ▪ €€€

The Vinothek at the Hotel Excelsior has a 500-bottle wine list to complement the kitchen's sophisticated cuisine.

9 Südtiroler Stuben

Diners at Alfons Schuhbeck's gastro temple (see p95) can enjoy Bavarian-Mediterranean cuisine.

10 Rue des Halles

Haishausen's oldest French establishment, this unpretentious brasserie (see p117) wouldn't look out of place among the old Parisian market halls. Innovative French cooking is offered here.

TOP 10 SPOTS FOR BREAKFAST AND BRUNCH

The elegant White Rabbit's Room

1 White Rabbit's Room
MAP Q5 ▪ Franziskanerstraße 19
▪ www.white-rabbits-room.de
Quaint café with great croissants.

2 Cafe and der Uni
MAP N1 ▪ Ludwigstraße 24
▪ www.cadu.de
This lively café in the university quarter serves breakfast till 10pm.

3 Speiserei Volksbad
MAP P4 ▪ Rosenheimer Straße 1
▪ www.speisereivolksbad.de
Art Nouveau-style café at the Müller'sches Volksbad.

4 Das Neuhausen
MAP D3 ▪ Blutenburgstraße 106
▪ www.dasneuhausen.de
Great breakfast selection.

5 Café Altschwabing
MAP M1 ▪ Schellingstraße 56
▪ www.altschwabing.com
Stucco decor, coffee-house ambience.

6 Aroma Kaffeebar
MAP M5 ▪ Pestalozzistraße 24
▪ www.aromakaffeebar.com
Breakfast, coffee and homemade cake served all day long.

7 Café am Beethovenplatz
Breakfast with live music (from 11am Sun), and a popular terrace (see p123).

8 Café Noel
MAP Q5 ▪ Metzstraße 8
Delicious cakes, sandwiches, light bites and a cosy atmosphere.

9 Tagträumer
MAP L6 ▪ Dreimühlenstraße 17
▪ www.tagtraum-muenchen.de
Fabulous weekend breakfasts.

10 Stenz
MAP K5 ▪ Lindwurmstraße 122
Breakfast with a Bavarian twist.

For a key to restaurant price ranges see p83

🔟 Beer Gardens

Chinesischer Turm

1 Chinesischer Turm
With 7,000 seats, the Chinese Tower *(see p23)* is one of the city's most famous landmarks, and is frequented by students, tourists and locals alike. Brass bands play on the first floor of the pagoda at the weekend. There is also a play area and an old wooden carousel nearby.

2 Taxisgarten
Karte C2
▪ **Taxisstraße 12**
This neighbourhood beer garden (1,500 capacity) in Neuhausen is a cosy spot sheltered by chestnut and ash trees.

Taxisgarten sign

3 Augustiner-Keller
MAP K2 ▪ **Arnulfstraße 52**
This vast beer garden shaded by ancient chestnut trees and located near a former place of execution has been in operation since the 19th century. There are 5,000 seats for guests, of which half have table service. About 200 decorated tables for the regulars add a whimsical note. There is also a play area. On warm summer evenings, this beer garden is packed. Don't miss the Augustiner Edelstoff on tap from wooden barrels.

4 Seehaus
A great place to people-watch, this popular beer garden *(see p23)* is at the centre of the Englischer Garten, right on the Kleinhesseloher See. It can accommodate 2,500 people, with 400 more on the stylish terrace. The beer garden (serving Paulaner) has a cosy atmosphere. Boats can be hired by the lake. There is also a play area.

5 Hofbräukeller
MAP Q4 ▪ **Innere Wiener Straße 19**
Across the Isar in Haidhausen, the Hofbräukeller – once the site of a brewery and its cellar – has been serving beer since 1892. There are 1,400 tables, of which 400 have table service. The dense canopy of chestnuts keeps drinkers comfortable and dry even on damp days. There is also a play area on the premises.

6 Hirschgarten
Munich's largest beer garden *(see p128)* seats 8,000 people and is next to Schloss Nymphenburg. Augustiner Edelstoff is served on tap from the huge wooden barrel, known as a "Hirsch".

7 Aumeister
Sondermeierstraße 1
This huge beer garden (3,000 capacity) on the north side of the Englischer Garten serves Hofbräu, along with a selection of seasonal

Foaming Bavarian beers

beers, including Starkbier in March, and Sommerbier and Wiesnbier during Oktoberfest. Parasols shelter drinkers on the Mediterranean terrace. There is also an adventure playground here.

Drinkers at the Viktualienmarkt

⑧ Biergarten am Viktualienmarkt

MAP N4 ■ Viktualienmarkt 9

Nestled between the market stalls of Viktualienmarkt, this centrally located beer garden seats 800 people, with table service for 200. The highlight of this place is that it serves beer from all of Munich's breweries on a six-week rotation. In the summer months, it hosts concerts by traditional bands on Sundays, and the Brunnenfest takes place on the first Friday in August under the watchful eye of the statue of the actor Weiß Ferdl.

⑨ Wirtshaus am Bavariapark

Chestnut trees shelter this beer garden and pub *(see p125)* in Bavariapark with capacity for 1,200 patrons (and a further 300 on the terrace). Augustiner is served here.

⑩ Zum Flaucher

MAP E6 ■ Isarauen 8

This idyllic beer garden (700 capacity) on the banks of the Isar is dotted with beautiful old trees. You're likely to come across sunbathers on the Isar beach, as well as cyclists and families with children. Löwenbräu is offered here. The garden also has a play area.

TOP 10 BAVARIAN BEERS

1 Augustiner
Brewed since 1328 in the monastery near the cathedral, under the purity law since 1516, Augustiner is regarded as the champagne of beers.

2 Franziskaner Weissbier
Franciscan friars have brewed this beer since 1363 in the former monastery on Residenzstraße. Now part of the Spaten-Löwenbräu Group.

3 Paulaner
Pauline monks in the Au began to brew beer as far back as 1634. The most famous master brewer was Brother Barnabas, and Salvator beer is still made using his 18th-century recipe.

4 Löwenbräu
Dating back to the 14th century, this is made in Munich's largest brewery.

5 Hofbräu
Duke Wilhelm V founded his own court brewery in 1589. A new fermenting site was set up on Platzl in 1607 – it is now known as the Hofbräuhaus.

6 Spaten
This brewery is named after the 16th-century Spatt family.

7 Hacker-Pschorr
The first recorded mention of this beer was in 1417. Today, it is part of the Paulaner Group.

8 Erdinger Weißbier
Erdinger is one of the top sellers among nearly 1,000 different types of Bavarian wheat beers.

9 Ayinger
This small brewery in Aying is home to a dozen well-known beers.

10 Andechser
Beer has been brewed at this Benedictine abbey on the "sacred mountain" since the Middle Ages.

Guests at the busy Andechser

Traditional Taverns

The façade of the Zum Franziskaner

1 Zum Franziskaner
MAP N3 ▪ Residenzstraße 9
▪ (089) 231 8120

This 200-year-old traditional pub is said to serve the best Leberkäse (meat loaf) in town. The Weißwürste (sausages) are highly recommended too.

2 Hofbräuhaus
You can't come to Munich and not pay a visit to the most famous beer hall (see p89) in the world.

3 Spatenhaus an der Oper
MAP N3 ▪ Residenzstraße 12
▪ (089) 290 7060

The ground floor of this traditional pub on Max-Joseph-Platz has a homely, unpretentious atmosphere, while the upper floor has a more sophisticated ambience. Diners come here to enjoy a menu of hearty Munich cooking.

Lion fountain, Hofbräuhaus

4 Schneider Bräuhaus
The former Weiße Bräuhaus offers traditional Munich fare, including Kronfleischküche (skirt steak dishes). Whether you opt for Kalbslüngerl (pickled lights of veal), Milzwurst (spleen sausage) or Schweinsbraten (roast pork), the food here (see p83) is outstanding.

A wheat bock beer called Aff is served on tap. Also, be sure to try the Schneider Weisse.

5 Wirtshaus in der Au
MAP P5 ▪ Lilienstraße 51 ▪ (089) 448 1400

The Wirtshaus, founded in 1901, is renowned for its dumplings, which include varieties containing either wild garlic, spinach or ham. Meat lovers might also want to try the duck, steak or ox fillet. Renowned dumpling-making courses are run by the owners for locals and visitors alike. Paulaner and Auer craft beer are served on tap.

6 Zum Augustiner
Housed in a traditional building that operated as a brewery until 1885, this large restaurant (see p83) has an interior that's well worth a look (particularly the mussel hall). In summer, there is outdoor seating in the paved pedestrian zone and in an arcaded courtyard.

Outdoor tables at Zum Augustiner

⑦ Löwenbräukeller
 MAP L2 ■ Stiglmaierplatz
■ (089) 5472 6690

This historic building complete with an exquisite taproom, a ceremonial hall and a large beer garden dominates the Stiglmaierplatz. It also serves as a venue for carnival balls and congresses, and plays host to the tapping of the first Triumphator barrel to welcome in the "fifth season" in March. A stone lion, the Löwenbräu emblem, sits majestically above the entrance.

Main hall at the Löwenbräukeller

⑧ Paulaner Bräuhaus
A cosy, homely pub (see p125) furnished with dark wood and brewing equipment. House-brewed Paulaner is, of course, served on tap. The game dishes in particular are excellent.

⑨ Fraunhofer
MAP M5 ■ Fraunhoferstraße 9
■ (089) 266460

Parts of this atmospheric tavern date back to when it was first built, in around 1900. It attracts a mix of locals and tourists and hosts weekly music sessions on Sunday mornings. Its courtyard is home to both a cabaret stage and the legendary Werkstattkino (see p57) cinema.

⑩ Augustiner Bräustuben
While Oktoberfest is in full swing, this (see p125) is the place to come for a glimpse of the brewery's show horses. Both the inn itself and the brewery's stables are brimming with traditional Bavarian charm.

TOP 10 TRADITIONS IN AND AROUND MUNICH

1 Schäfflertanz
Munich, Carnival
This dance of the Schäffler takes place every seven years (next in 2026) to commemorate the end of the plague.

2 Tanz der Marktfrauen
Munich, Shrove Tue
Women at the Viktualienmarkt stalls dance in colourful costumes.

3 Starkbierzeit
Bavaria, St Joseph's Day (19 Mar) until Easter
Celebrating the "fifth season of the year" by tapping barrels of potent Starkbier.

4 Maibaum
Bavaria, 1 May
The day to set up the maypole.

5 Fronleichnamsprozession
Thu after Trinity Sunday
Processions for the Feast of Corpus Christi take place across South Bavaria, the largest running through Munich.

6 Kocherlball
Third Sun in Jul
Costumed couples dance the Ländler, Zwiefacher and Polka to pay homage to the servants who once did the same.

7 Trachten
Witness local costumes (Trachten) in the region's processions and festivals.

8 Christkindlmärkte
Bavaria, first day of advent until 24 Dec
Christmas markets in Marienplatz.

9 Alphornblasen, Jodeln and Schuhplatteln
Alphorns, yodelling and the thigh-slapping Schuhplatteln dance.

10 Leonhardi-Umzüge
Upper Bavaria, first Sunday in Nov
Processions in honour of St Leonhard, patron saint of horses.

Horses in the Leonhardi-Umzug

Shopping

1 Theatinerstraße and Residenzstraße
MAP N3

Theatinerstraße begins at Marienhof, behind the Neues Rathaus. This shopping street is home to fashion boutiques, high-end stores and the Fünf Höfe shopping centre. If you're looking for luxury brands, head for Residenzstraße, which runs parallel to Theatinerstraße.

2 Fünf Höfe
MAP N3 ■ www.fuenfhoefe.de

Historic buildings and contemporary architecture, arcades, courtyards, shops, culture and fine gastronomy – this award-winning example of urban design by architects Herzog & de Meuron covers the area between Theatinerstraße, Kardinal-Faulhaber-Straße, Maffeistraße and Salvatorstraße.

3 Sendlinger Straße and HOFSTATT
MAP M4 ■ www.hofstatt.info

Sendlinger Straße is one of the oldest shopping streets in Munich and has several traditional stores, although it is becoming increasingly chic. Its latest addition is HOFSTATT, a shopping mall with popular chains such as Hollister, Gant, Mango and Calzedonia.

The modern HOFSTATT arcade

Kaufingerstraße at dusk

4 Pedestrian Zone
MAP M3

Munich's central pedestrian zone stretches along Kaufingerstraße and Neuhauser Straße to Karlsplatz/Stachus. This is the busiest street in the whole city, with several places of interest interspersed among the retail frenzy.

5 Maximilianstraße and Maximilianhöfe
MAP N3 ■ www.maximilianhoefe.de

This elegant 19th-century boulevard between the Nationaltheater and Altstadtring is one of the most exclusive retail destinations in Europe. Armani, Bulgari and Gucci are just some of the names that beckon from this shopping street designed in the "Maximilianstil" of the era by Friedrich Bürklein. The Maximilianhöfe complex (including brands such as Gianfranco Ferré and Dolce & Gabbana) attracts shoppers with money to burn.

6 Around Viktualienmarkt
MAP N4

Worth a stroll whether you're shopping or not, Viktualienmarkt (see p80) is surrounded by speciality stores of all sizes. Small antiques shops and the largest organic supermarket in the city line the narrow streets leading to the Isartor. A shopping arcade runs in the direction of Rindermarkt and the Löwenturm.

7 Around the University
MAP N1

Bounded by the Amalienstraße, Schellingstraße, Türkenstraße and Adalbertstraße, the student quarter features not only the bookshops you might expect, but also chic boutiques, jewellery stores and trendy design shops.

8 Leopoldstraße and Hohenzollernstraße
MAP FG2–3

Starting from the top of Giselastraße, Schwabing's Leopoldstraße is lined with shops, restaurants and cafés. Stroll along the side streets on the left-hand side of the boulevard (heading away from the centre), especially Hohenzollernstraße, for a wide variety of shops.

9 Around Gärtnerplatz
MAP N4–5

In addition to its popular cafés, bars and restaurants, the scenic Gärtnerplatz quarter is home to a whole host of specialist shops, such as Blutsgeschwister with its own fashion line.

Blutsgeschwister in the Gärtnerplatz

10 Shopping Centres

Major shopping centres outside central Munich are the OEZ (Olympia-Einkaufszentrum), Pasing Arcaden by the S-Bahn station, Riem Arcaden in the exhibition city of Riem, and the Einkaufs-Center Neuperlach.

TOP 10 MARKETS AND FAIRS

Fresh produce at Viktualienmarkt

1 Viktualienmarkt
Established in 1807, Viktualienmarkt (see p80) is a top destination for foodies.

2 Elisabethmarkt
MAP F3
This market on Elisabethplatz is the second largest in Munich.

3 Wiener Markt
MAP Q4
The old market stalls here are often used as a set for films and TV shows.

4 Großmarkthalle
MAP E6
Munich wholesale market is full of atmosphere.

5 Auer Dulten
MAP P6 ▪ Mariahilfplatz
▪ www.auerdult.de
Three nine-day fairs run from the end of April, July and mid-October.

6 Antikmärkte
Flohmarkt München Daglfing and the open-air flea market at the Zenith exhibition centre are both brimming with trash, treasures and antiques.

7 Trödelmärkte and Flohmärkte
The city's largest flea markets are the Riesen-Flohmarkt on Theresienwiese and Flohmarkt München-Riem.

8 Hinterhofflohmärkte
www.hofflohmaerkte.de/muenchen
Many districts across the city hold their own backyard jumble sales.

9 Münchner Christkindlmarkt
The largest Christmas market is held in Marienplatz. If you're looking for more atmosphere, try those in the Schwabing and Haidhausen districts.

10 Magdalenenfest
MAP H2 ▪ Hirschgarten
A small July folk festival with a market.

Munich for Free

 Surfers on the Eisbach
The crowds on the bridge next to the Haus der Kunst can usually be seen from afar. What they've come to see are the surfers who ride the artificial wave created in the Eisbach stream *(see p22)* all year round.

Surfers on the Eisbach rapids

2 Gasteig HP8
During the multi-year renovation of the Gasteig *(see p112)* in Haidhausen, events – including free concerts, exhibitions, readings and courses – will take place in the Gasteig HP8.

3 BMW Welt
The dynamic architecture of this futuristic building *(see p129)* with its striking double cone entrance makes it well worth a visit. Exhibitions are free to enter.

The double cone at BMW Welt

4 Glockenspiel
The famous Glockenspiel *(see p12)* chiming clock in the alcoves of the Neues Rathaus springs into action every day at 11am and noon (and again at 5pm in summer). The top section depicts the wedding of Duke Wilhelm V and Renate von Lothringen with a jousting tournament. Beneath them is the coopers' dance.

5 Museums and Galleries
The Museum für Abgüsse Klassischer Bildwerke (Katharina-von-Bora-Straße 10), Geologisches Museum (Luisenstraße 37), Kartoffelmuseum (Grafinger Straße 2), Feuerwehrmuseum (An der Hauptfeuerwache 8) and Lothringer 13 *(see p45)* all offer free admission. A number of other major museums (including the Pinakotheken) are also free for under-18s.

6 Olympiapark
While many of the attractions at Olympiapark *(see pp32–3)* have an entry fee, it doesn't cost a thing to wander the site, admiring the 1970s architecture of various Olympic venues. For fans of fireworks, the Sommernachtstraum (Midsummer Night's Dream) event in July puts on a spectacular display. You can even pack up a picnic and listen from inside the park whenever major concerts take place at the stadium.

Free concert at Theatron

⑦ Theatron

At Whitsuntide and for three weeks in the summer, free concerts (see p75) are held at the amphitheatre in Olympiapark.

⑧ Training at FC Bayern
www.fcbayern.com/shop

Experience a training session with the masters: fans can visit the stadium on Säbener Straße 51 to get up close and personal with their football heroes and maybe even bag an autograph. Dates of public training sessions are available on the club shop's website.

⑨ Open-Air Performances
www.muenchner-sommer
theater.de

The Gärtnerplatztheater orchestra plays a free concert at the Gärtner-platzfest in July. In summer and autumn, the Mohr-Villa on the north side of the Englischer Garten stage classic plays (see website for details). "Oper für alle" puts on a live transmission of an opera performance on Max-Joseph-Platz and a free festival concert on Marstallplatz in July.

⑩ Observatory at the Deutsches Museum

Excellent free tours of the observatory at the Deutsches Museum (see pp26–7) are available every Tuesday and Friday evening.

TOP 10 BUDGET TIPS

1 MVV Group Tickets
The MVV (Munich Traffic and Tariff Association) offers cheap group tickets for up to five adults (children count as half an adult).

2 CityTourCard
For regular users of public transport, the CityTourCard (see p141) also offers discounts on over 60 attractions.

3 Sightseeing by Tram
Take the scenic route: Tram 19 passes by Lenbachplatz, along Maximilianstraße, and across the Isar to Haidhausen – all for the price of a regular tram ticket.

4 Discovering the City on a Bike
MVG Rad (see p141) is the name of the city's cycle-hire system – a great, inexpensive way to discover Munich.

5 Museums for a Euro
The state museums, along with some others, offer entry to the permanent exhibitions for just €1 on Sundays.

6 Sunset on the Terrace
You don't have to go to an expensive rooftop bar: the roof terrace of the café at Vorhoelzer Forum (see p101) has a great view and reasonably priced drinks.

7 Fine Dining on a Shoestring
Many gourmet restaurants – even some with Michelin stars – have extremely reasonable lunch menus.

8 District Festivals
These events usually offer free entertainment and cheap food.

9 Picnic in the Beer Garden
You can take your own snacks to any beer garden and just pay for drinks.

10 Kinotag
For cut-price movie tickets, Kinotag (cinema day) is on Mondays (also Tuesdays in some cinemas).

Kinotag at the City Kinos

Festivals and Open-Air Events

1 Dance

Every 2 years in May (2023, 2025) ■ www.dance-muenchen.de

This innovative dance festival takes place at about ten different venues around the city, including the Gasteig and Residenztheater.

Crowds at the Streetlife Festival

2 Streetlife Festival

May/Jun & Sep ■ www.street life-festival.de

This sustainability festival organized by Green City takes place over two weekends a year. Leopoldstraße and Ludwigstraße are closed off to traffic as food and drink vendors take over the streets.

3 Münchener Biennale

Every 2 years in May/Jun (2024, 2026) ■ (089) 2805607 ■ www.muenchenerbiennale.de

The first of its kind in the world, this musical theatre festival was founded in 1988 by composer Hans Werner Henze (1926–2012). The city of Munich commissions young composers to write their first full work for the festival.

Now a biennial event, the festival has become an established fixture with a diverse programme.

4 Filmfest

Smaller than the Berlin festival and not quite as star-studded, this film festival (see p56) has made a name for itself as a festival of the people.

5 Opernfestspiele

End Jun–end Jul ■ www.bayerische.staatsoper.de

Under Ludwig II, Munich grew into a centre of music, and it was the site of premieres of Wagner's operas and of a major Mozart festival. In 1910, the Richard Strauss festival week was launched, a tradition continued in the Opernfestspiele (Munich Opera Festival), which features both classic works and contemporary pieces. Free "Opera for all" performances are also held.

6 Tollwood

Summer festival (Jun/Jul) in Olympiapark South, winter festival (Nov–New Year) at Theresienwiese ■ (0700) 3838 5024 (tickets) ■ www.tollwood.de

A bi-annual music, dance and theatre festival, held in summer and winter. Formerly an alternative event, it has matured into a major festival with a wide-ranging programme of performances, vendors and organic foods.

Tollwood festival at night

⑦ Königsplatz Open Air
Jul–Aug ▪ www.kinoopenair.de

The backdrop of the Königsplatz seems tailor-made for open-air events. In summer, you can enjoy a wide variety of concerts here, ranging from classical to rock and pop. The large square is also used for open-air film screenings.

⑧ Theatron Musiksommer and PfingstFestival
Whitsun, Aug ▪ www.theatron.de

At Whitsuntide, as well as for 24 days during the summer, the amphitheatre at Olympiapark hosts a variety of musical events. The programme features artists from around the globe, and there's a real laid-back vibe about the whole event.

Visitors at the Oktoberfest

⑨ Oktoberfest
The largest beer festival in the world *(see pp34–5)* runs in Munich for 16 or 17 days, ending on the first Sunday of October.

⑩ SpielArt
Every 2 years in Oct & Nov (2023, 2025) ▪ www.spielart.org

Munich's "window on the world of theatre" presents new productions from around the world at various venues, usually with a focus on one country.

TOP 10 OTHER EVENTS

Performers at BallettFestwoche

1 BallettFestwoche
Apr ▪ www.bayerische.staatsoper.de
In-house productions by the Staatsballett with guest performances.

2 Frühlingsfest
Mid-Apr–start of May
The Oktoberfest's little sister, held on the Theresienwiese.

3 DOK.fest München
Watch international documentary films, premieres and work from up-and-coming directors *(see p57)*.

4 Stadtgründungsfest
Weekend closest to 2 June
A cultural programme between Marienplatz and Odeonsplatz.

5 Brunnenhofkonzerte
Jun–Aug ▪ www.muenchen.de
Enjoy classical music, tango, movie scores and many other genres at the Residenz on warm summer nights.

6 Krimifestival
Spring and autumn ▪ www. krimifestival-muenchen.de
International crime thriller authors visit the Isar to perform readings.

7 Christopher Street Day
Jul ▪ www.csdmuenchen.de
Parade and show programme put on by the LGBTQ+ community.

8 Fantasy Filmfest
Horror films, thrillers and more *(see p57)*.

9 Stadtteilwochen
Summer, individual districts
Each district puts on its own week-long festival with food and cultural events.

10 Lange Nächte
May & Oct ▪ www.muenchner.de
The "long night" of music is held in the summer; the equivalent event for museums happens later in the year.

Munich Area by Area

Panoramic view of Central Munich

TOP 10 Southern Old Town

Three of Munich's original city gates still stand, marking the boundaries of the southern old town: the Karlstor on Stachus, Sendlinger Tor and Isartor. Right at the centre of the old town is Marienplatz, Munich's main square. A former grain and salt market, it is now a key transport hub and a popular meeting place for locals. This part of the old town is also home to most of the city's shopping areas and pedestrian zones, as well as the Viktualienmarkt. Some of the oldest buildings in the city can be found in this part of Munich.

Virgin and Child, Mariensäule

Main altar of the Peterskirche

1 Peterskirche
MAP N4 ▪ Rindermarkt 1
▪ Tower: open 9am–6:30pm Mon–Fri, 10am–7pm Sat & Sun (winter: until 6pm) ▪ Adm

The oldest church (see p12) in the city dates back to the 12th century, although it has undergone a number of stylistic renovations since. A gilded

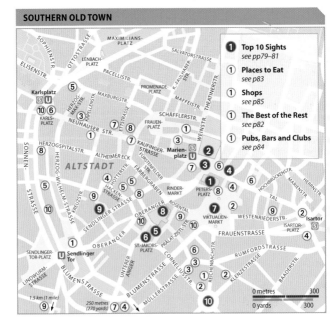

SOUTHERN OLD TOWN

- **1** Top 10 Sights
  see pp79–81
- **1** Places to Eat
  see p83
- **1** Shops
  see p85
- **1** The Best of the Rest
  see p82
- **1** Pubs, Bars and Clubs
  see p84

0 metres 300
0 yards 300

figure of St Peter stands in the middle of the main altar and the remains of St Munditia are on display in a glass coffin. The view from the 91-m (299-ft) high tower is spectacular.

Vaulted ceiling in the Neues Rathaus

② Neues Rathaus
MAP N3

The magnificent Neo-Gothic New Town Hall *(see pp12–13)* was built by Georg Hauberrisser between 1867 and 1909 and is home to the mayor's office. Ninety-minute guided tours of the building run on three days a week – a lift takes visitors up to the 85-m (279-ft) high observation deck in the tower. At the top of the tower sits the city's mascot, the Münchner Kindl (a young monk). The Rathaus draws a crowd at least twice a day when its Glockenspiel starts to chime (at 11am and noon, also at 5pm in summer).

③ Marienplatz
MAP N3–4

Munich's main square *(see pp12–13)* is dominated by the Neues Rathaus, while its eastern side is bounded by the Gothic Altes Rathaus. Both the Mariensäule and the Fischbrunnen are popular meeting spots, the latter dating back to the Middle Ages. Every year on Ash Wednesday, the fountain is the site of a traditional ceremony that started back in 1426: Geldbeutel-waschen, when the mayor and city councillors wash empty money bags for good luck. Marienplatz is a hive of activity, playing host to festivals, demonstrations, and FC Bayern celebrations (trophies are presented from the town hall balcony).

④ Altes Rathaus
MAP N4

Construction of the Gothic Old Town Hall *(see p12)* on Marienplatz started in 1470 under architect Jörg von Halspach. The building was the seat of the city council until 1874 and is still a popular venue for official events; its ceremonial hall has a reconstructed late Gothic barrel vault and is adorned with coats of arms. Once the city administration had relocated to the Neues Rathaus, the ground floor was converted to create a drive-through and a separate pedestrian passage on to Tal. The Altes Rathaus tower is now home to a toy museum.

Restored façade of the Altes Rathaus

Exterior of Synagoge Ohel Jakob

5 Synagoge Ohel Jakob

MAP M4 ■ St-Jakobs-Platz 18 ■ Tours: www.juedisches-museum muenchen.de

Munich's main synagogue, Ohel Jakob, was unveiled in November 2006. Its design, by architects Wandel Höfer Lorch, features two stacked cubes: a solid travertine base topped with a delicate glass structure and a metallic grid. The synagogue is the jewel in the crown of an ensemble comprising the Jewish Museum and a community centre. Access to the building is via an underground Corridor of Remembrance from the community centre.

6 Jüdisches Museum München

MAP M4 ■ St-Jakobs-Platz 16 ■ (089) 2339 6096 ■ Open 10am–6pm Tue–Sun ■ Adm ■ www. juedisches-museum-muenchen.de

This freestanding cube of a museum with its wraparound glazing presents Jewish history and culture in Munich as part of its permanent exhibition, titled "Stimmen – Orte – Zeiten" (Voices – Places – Times). It also puts on temporary exhibitions.

7 Viktualienmarkt

MAP N4 ■ Open 7am–8pm Mon–Sat

Viktualienmarkt exudes a unique atmosphere. This former farmers' market has become a real foodie destination, but it doesn't come cheap. The market has its own beer garden, as well as six fountains featuring local figures. Shrove Tuesday is always a great spectacle, when women come out from their stalls to take part in the famous "Tanz der Marktfrauen" (Dance of the Market Women). At the southernmost end of the market is Der Pschorr restaurant (see p83) and the reconstructed Schrannenhalle from 1853, which is home to the popular deli chain, Eataly.

8 Münchner Stadtmuseum

MAP M4 ■ St-Jakobs-Platz 1 ■ (089) 2332 2370 ■ Open 10am–6pm Tue–Sun ■ Adm ■ www. muenchner-stadtmuseum.de

This museum (see p44) occupies a number of buildings and documents the history and culture of the city across four permanent exhibitions. Some of the highlights include the Morris Dancers sculpture by Erasmus Grasser, the special exhibit looking at Munich's role in the rise of the Nazis, and the film museum (see p56).

Costume (c.1840), Münchner Stadtmuseum

9 Asamkirche and Asam-Haus

MAP M4 ■ Sendlinger Straße 32–34 ■ Church: open 9am–5pm daily

Between 1729 and 1733, Egid Quirin Asam purchased four separate properties on Sendlinger Straße. This is where he built his extensively stuccoed residence and – together with his brother Cosmas Damian – the Asamkirche (Church of St John of Nepomuk) of 1733. This late Baroque structure *(see p42)* was intended to be a private church (it offered a direct view of the high altar from the Asam-Haus), but the city council refused to grant a construction permit until the brothers agreed to make it accessible to the public. Sandwiched between the houses, the church has no surface left unadorned. It overflows with cherubs and barley-sugar columns, false marble and stucco, frescos and oil paintings. The hidden windows of the interior let in only a little light, which evokes an almost mystical atmosphere.

Aerial view of the Gärtnerplatz

🔟 Gärtnerplatz
MAP N4–5

This hexagonal square was laid out in 1860 and named to commemorate the German architect Friedrich von Gärtner. Its central fountain and flower beds lend it something of a Mediterranean feel. At the square's southern end is the Neo-Classical Staatstheater am Gärtnerplatz *(see p55)*, a theatre dating from 1865. The square now sits at the heart of the Gärtnerplatz quarter *(see p71)*, renowned for its shops, restaurants and numerous cafés. The area is also home to Munich's LGBTQ+ scene, along with the neighbouring Glockenbach quarter.

A DAY IN THE SOUTHERN OLD TOWN

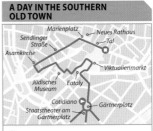

▶ MORNING

Start the day with a coffee in **Cotidiano** *(Gärtnerplatz 6)* with a view of the **Staatstheater am Gärtnerplatz** and its namesake square. From here, take a stroll down the streets that lead away from **Gärtnerplatz** in a star shape and explore the many little shops and boutiques of the area. When you reach Rumfordstraße, take a left onto Utzschneiderstraße and you'll see the Schrannenhalle right ahead, which is now a branch of the Italian deli chain, **Eataly**. You can either buy a snack here or wait and check out the wide selection on offer at **Viktualienmarkt**. Here you can enjoy lunch in the beer garden, with a great view of the maypole in the middle of the square.

AFTERNOON

Once you've refuelled, head down Prälat-Zistl-Straße and turn right onto St-Jakobs-Platz to reach the boldly designed, modern synagogue, the **Jüdisches Museum** and the Münchner Stadtmuseum. Be sure to visit the "Typisch München" (Typical Munich) exhibit at the Stadtmuseum. Next, walk down Oberanger, taking a right turn onto Schmidstraße towards **Sendlinger Straße**. This is where you will find the incredible piece of Baroque that is the **Asamkirche** and Asam-Haus. Now head north as far as **Marienplatz**, where the famous Glockenspiel attraction awaits you at the **Neues Rathaus** at 5pm (Mar–Oct). Try to find a spot for dinner in one of the busy restaurants along **Tal** or around the Viktualienmarkt.

See map on p78 ←

The Best of the Rest

1 Sendlinger Tor
MAP M4

This city gate (Stadttor) from 1318 is overgrown with wild vines and marks the southern entrance to Sendlinger Straße.

2 Isartor
MAP N4 ■ Tal 50 ■ (089) 223266 ■ Open 11am–6pm Thu–Tue ■ Adm ■ www.valentin-musaeum.de

The Valentin-Karlstadt-Musäum in the south tower of the Isartor is devoted to cabaret artists Karl Valentin and Liesl Karlstadt. The Turmstüberl (museum café) is furnished in *fin-de-siècle* style.

3 Bürgersaalkirche
MAP M3 ■ Neuhauser Straße 14

The Bürgersaal (community hall) has been used as a church by the Sodality of Our Lady since 1778.

4 Heiliggeistkirche
This Viktualienmarkt church (see p43) is one of the city's oldest.

Heiliggeistkirche on Viktualienmarkt

5 Künstlerhaus
MAP M3 ■ Lenbachplatz 8

The Künstlerhaus (House of Artists) on Lenbachplatz was once a meeting place for artists and Munich society. It now hosts cultural events.

The Karlstor city gate

6 Karlstor and Stachus
MAP M3

Karlsplatz/Stachus, with its fountains and the medieval Karlstor, marks the end of the pedestrian zone.

7 Michaelskirche
This Jesuit church (see p42) in the pedestrian zone is a prime example of Renaissance architecture.

8 Deutsches Jagd- und Fischereimuseum
MAP M3 ■ Neuhauser Straße 2 ■ (089) 220522 ■ Open 9:30am–5pm Thu–Sun ■ Adm ■ www.jagd-fischerei-museum.de

Hunting and fishing displays, including jackalope-type creations, in the former Augustinerkirche.

9 Bier- und Oktoberfestmuseum
MAP N4 ■ Sterneckerstraße 2 ■ (089) 2423 1607 ■ Open 1–6pm Tue–Sat ■ Adm ■ www.bier-und-oktoberfestmuseum.de

Housed in a medieval building, this museum presents Munich's history of beer along with everything you need to know about Oktoberfest.

10 Ignaz-Günther-Haus
MAP M4 ■ St-Jakobs-Platz 20

This 16th-century late Gothic house was the home and studio of sculptor Ignaz Günther (1725–75).

Places to Eat

PRICE CATEGORIES

Price of a three-course meal (or similar) for one with a glass of wine or beer, including taxes and service.

€ below €30   €€ €30–60   €€€ over €60

1 Zum Augustiner
MAP M3 ■ Neuhauser Straße 27 ■ (089) 2318 3257 ■ €

A local Bavarian favourite, Zum Augustiner has a mussel hall and an arcaded garden.

2 Bratwurstherzl
MAP N4 ■ Dreifaltigkeitsplatz 1 ■ (089) 295113 ■ Closed Sun ■ €

Bavarian classics such as *Saueres Kalbslüngerl* (pickled veal's lung) or *Saure Zipfel* (pickled sausage) are served here.

3 Nürnberger Bratwurst Glöckl am Dom
MAP M3 ■ Frauenplatz 9 ■ (089) 291945 ■ www.bratwurst-gloeckl.de ■ €

Among the dishes on offer here is the famous *Rostbratwürste mit Kraut* (barbecued sausages with cabbage).

4 Landersdorfer and Innerhofer
MAP M4 ■ Hackenstraße 6–8 ■ (089) 2601 8637 ■ Closed Sat & Sun ■ www.landersdorferund innerhofer.de ■ €€€

This traditional restaurant *(see p64)* has an extensive wine list, set menus and a convivial atmosphere.

5 Prinz Myshkin
MAP M4 ■ Hackenstraße 2 ■ (089) 265596 ■ €

Creative vegan and vegetarian cuisine is served in an elegant setting beneath high vaulted ceilings at Prinz Myshkin *(see p63)*.

Salad with sesame sauce at Prinz Myshkin

6 Schneider Bräuhaus
MAP N4 ■ Tal 7 ■ (089) 290 1380 ■ www.schneider-brauhaus.de ■ €

The flavours of Munich are at their best here: offal, sausage and roast pork served with cold Schneider Weisse beer.

The corner of Schneider Bräuhaus

7 Café Glockenspiel
MAP N3 ■ Marienplatz 28 (entrance on Rosenstraße) ■ (089) 264256 ■ €€

Offering homemade cakes by day and international cuisine at night.

8 Café Rischart
MAP N4 ■ Viktualienmarkt 2 ■ (089) 231 700330 ■ €

This café has a terrace with beautiful views. Its flagship branch can be found on Marienplatz.

9 Café Frischhut
MAP N4 ■ Prälat-Zistl-Straße 8 ■ (089) 268237

The only items on the menu here *(see p60)* are doughnuts and pastries, which are prepared in front of you and served with hot drinks.

10 Der Pschorr
MAP N4 ■ Viktualienmarkt 15 ■ (089) 44238 3940 ■ €€

From its restaurant, beer garden and terrace, Der Pschorr offers Bavarian cuisine and traditional beer culture.

See map on p78 ←

Pubs, Bars and Clubs

Performance at Kilians Irish Pub

1 Kilians Irish Pub
MAP N3 ▪ Frauenplatz 11
▪ (089) 2421 9899

A pub (see p61), complete with Irish stew on the menu, Guinness, and live music. There is karaoke every Sunday.

2 Niederlassung
MAP N4 ▪ Buttermelcherstraße 6 ▪ (089) 3260 0307 ▪ Closed Mon

This quaint, cosy pub has an excellent gin selection (over 60 different types). Happy hours for cocktails are from 7 to 9pm and again after midnight.

3 Paradiso Tanzbar
MAP N4 ▪ Rumfordstraße 2
▪ Open from 10pm Fri & Sat
▪ www.paradiso-tanzbar.de

This opulent club (see p58) with red velvet, mirrors and crystal chandeliers, served as the back-drop for Freddie Mercury's Living on My Own.

4 Zephyr Bar
MAP N5 ▪ Baaderstraße 68
▪ Closed Sun

One of the many bars in this area, Zephyr (see p60) is a long-standing favourite among locals.

5 Café Kranich
MAP L4 ▪ Sonnenstraße 19
▪ Open daily ▪ www.cafe-kranich.de

This stylish café has a large, attractive terrace. Food on offer includes burgers (vegetarian options available) and healthy salads.

6 Buena Vista Bar
MAP N4 ▪ Am Einlass 2a
▪ Closed Mon ▪ www.buena-vista-bar.de

Friendly Cuban bar serving tasty cocktails and tapas.

7 Flushing Meadows
MAP M5 ▪ Fraunhoferstraße 32
▪ (089) 5527 9170

Visit this rooftop bar (see p60) for great drinks, spectacular views and a relaxed atmosphere.

8 Bohne & Malz
MAP M3 ▪ Sonnenstraße 11
▪ (089) 557179

This pub, which has outdoor seating, serves breakfasts, Mediterranean-style dishes and cocktails.

9 Bahnwärter Thiel
MAP L4 ▪ Tumblingerstraße 45
▪ Opening hours vary, check website
▪ www.bahnwaerterthiel.de

Set against a backdrop of shipping containers and subway cars, this alternative arts centre hosts stand-up comedy and late-night DJ sets.

10 Milchbar
MAP M4 ▪ Sonnenstraße 27
▪ Open from 10pm Mon–Thu, from 11pm Fri & Sat ▪ www.milchundbar.de

Fans of house and electro flock here for the DJ sets. Start the week with the regular Blue Monday 1980s party.

Bar Dahoam at Milchbar

Shops

① Kauf Dich Glücklich
MAP N4 ■ Reichenbach-straße 14

One of two branches in Munich offering the latest trends from niche clothes designers to well-known brands. Also sells a selection of shoes, music and gifts.

② Blutsgeschwister
MAP N4 ■ Gärtnerplatz 6

Each branch of this chain has its own unique name, with this flagship outlet in Munich known as "German Schickeria". Occupying a prime position on Gärtnerplatz, it sells a range of women's clothing and accessories.

Blutsgeschwister's in Munich

③ CHI*KA so kind
MAP N4 ■ Müllerstraße 1

This store is brimming with items for children that have been lovingly selected, including organic children's and baby clothes from boutique design workshops, innovative and educational toys, and much more.

④ Globetrotter
MAP N4 ■ Isartorplatz 8–10

Lovers of the great outdoors need to look no further: everything you could possibly want or need is right here, along with a canoe testing pool, cold room, a climbing wall and a children's play area.

HOFSTATT arcade

⑤ HOFSTATT
MAP M4 ■ Sendlinger Straße 10

Once the home of the *Süddeutsche Zeitung* newspaper, this shopping mall has its own inner courtyards and sells fashion, accessories, cosmetics and food.

⑥ Ludwig Beck
MAP N3 ■ Marienplatz 11

Otherwise known as "Store of the Senses", this shop is in a league of its own for fashion, lingerie, stationery and music.

⑦ Kaufingerstraße and Neuhauser Straße
MAP M3

This pedestrian zone *(see p70)* is Munich's biggest shopping street.

⑧ Sendlinger Straße
MAP M4

This traditional shopping street is now home to the modern HOFSTATT – a shopping mall.

⑨ Servus Heimat
MAP M4 ■ Brunnstraße 3

Not your average souvenir shop, this place specializes in fun trinkets for Bayern fans.

⑩ Stachus-Passagen
MAP M3 ■ Karlsplatz

There are nearly 60 shops and restaurants occupying the lower floor of the S-Bahn.

See map on p78

TOP 10 Northern Old Town

Some of Munich's most important sights are clustered in the northern part of the old town. Extending north from Marienplatz as far as the top of the Altstadtring, this area includes the Frauenkirche and Theatinerkirche, as well as the Residenz palace complex and its Hofgarten. There are plenty of other sights too, including the long Promenadeplatz and its monuments, the Maximiliansplatz (one of the city's nightlife hubs), the Hotel Bayerischer Hof, and Odeonsplatz – once home to the Schwabinger Tor. This formed part of the second set of town ramparts, until the gate was torn down in 1817 to create the junction between Odeonsplatz and Ludwigstraße. In spite of all these attractions, it is a somewhat smaller square that is better known by far: Platzl, which is home to the world's most famous beer hall, the Hofbräuhaus.

The towers of the Frauenkirche

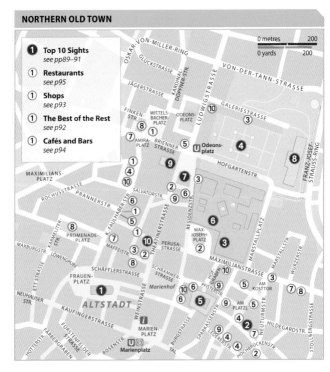

NORTHERN OLD TOWN

1 **Top 10 Sights**
see pp89–91

1 **Restaurants**
see p95

1 **Shops**
see p93

1 **The Best of the Rest**
see p92

1 **Cafés and Bars**
see p94

① Frauenkirche
MAP M3

Visible from much of the city centre, the Frauenkirche's twin towers dominate the Munich skyline. The design for this enormous church (see pp14–15) originally included Gothic spires, but unfortunately there was not enough money left to build them. It was not until 36 years later that the Frauenkirche's domes were added, and these would effectively become the model for all subsequent Bavarian onion domes.

② Platzl and Hofbräuhaus
MAP N3 ◼ Am Platzl 9 ◼ (089) 2 9013 6100 ◼ www.hofbraeuhaus.de

Munich and beer go back a long way: the Hofbräuhaus (1897) originated from a brewery (Hofbräu) founded by Wilhelm V in 1589. To this day, Hofbräu remains a Bavarian brand. The pub offers space for a thousand drinkers in its ground-floor bar, while the first floor is home to a ceremonial hall with a barrel vault ceiling, as well as a quieter bar. Outside the building itself, the Hofbräuhaus has an attractive beer garden sheltered by chestnut trees. It goes without saying that Hofbräu is served on tap – around 10,000 litres (21,134 US pints) a day, in fact. Away from the beer hall, the winding side streets that run off Platzl are the oldest part of Munich.

The new Residenztheater building

③ Nationaltheater and Residenztheater
MAP N3 ◼ Nationaltheater: Max-Joseph-Platz 2; (089) 2185 1920; www.staatsoper.de ◼ Residenztheater: Max-Joseph-Platz 1; (089) 2185 1940; www.residenztheater.de

The Nationaltheater has been the home of opera in Munich since it opened in 1818. It is also home to the state orchestra and ballet. The Opernfestspiele (see p74) brings fans here from around the world. After the destruction of the Residenztheater in World War II, a new building (see p54) was constructed between the Residenz and Nationaltheater. It is home to the Bavarian State Theatre, which sets the standard for German-language productions.

Interior of the Hofbräuhaus, the world's most famous beer hall

The Temple of Diana in the Hofgarten

4 Hofgarten
MAP N2–3

Head through the Hofgarten *(see p17)* archway on Odeonsplatz to reach the Renaissance garden, which was established while the Residenz was undergoing its extension work.

5 Alter Hof
MAP N3 ■ Burgstraße 4 ■ Open 10am–6pm Mon–Sat

Situated to the northeast of Marienhof (behind the Neues Rathaus), the Alter Hof is best reached via an archway among the old townhouses on Burgstraße. The first Residenz of the Wittelsbachs within the city walls was built between 1253 and 1255. Original features include the west wing, which has its own gatehouse adorned with coats of arms, and a tower-like bay window known as the Affenturm (monkey's tower). Legend has it

that the court monkey kidnapped Ludwig IV (who would later become emperor of Germany), and climbed with him to the top of the turret. Fortunately, the boy was soon brought back safe and sound by the monkey. The vaulted cellar of the Alter Hof contains a permanent exhibition on Bavarian castles, which includes information on the former Residenz.

6 Residenz
MAP N3

Munich's must-see palace *(see pp16–17)* was built over the centuries as a city-centre residence for the Wittelsbach rulers of Bavaria, after they outgrew the Alter Hof.

7 Feldherrnhalle
MAP N3 ■ Odeonsplatz

Ludwig I commissioned Friedrich von Gärtner to build the Feldherrnhalle at the south end of Odeonsplatz, based on the Loggia dei Lanzi in Florence, and it was completed in 1844. The statues here represent the Bavarian Feldherren (generals), the Count of Tilly and Baron von Wrede. The entrance steps are guarded by two lions. The building is not open to the public and can only be viewed from the outside.

8 Staatskanzlei
MAP N2–3 ■ Franz-Josef-Strauß-Ring 1 ■ Tours: Mon–Fri ■ Reservations: (089) 2165 2450

The Bayerische Staatskanzlei (Bavarian State Chancellery;

Bayerische Staatskanzlei, the Bavarian State Chancellery

1993), behind the Hofgarten, was the source of much controversy due to its ultra-modern design. Today, the complex combines the renovated cupola of the former army museum and a modern glass construction that was built over other historical structures.

The Baroque-Rococo Theatinerkirche

⑨ Theatinerkirche

MAP N3 ■ **Theatinerstraße 22** ■ **Open daily** ■ **Fürstengruft crypt: open May–Oct: 11:30am–3pm Mon–Sat** ■ **www.theatinerkirche.de**

Construction of the St Catejan court church, better known to locals as the Theatinerkirche (see p43), was begun in 1663 by Agostino Barelli. Enrico Zuccalli took over the project in 1674, and it was a good 100 years before François de Cuvilliés designed the Rococo façade. The crypt is the final resting place of the Wittelsbachs.

⑩ Kunsthalle der Hypo-Kulturstiftung

MAP N3 ■ **Theatinerstraße 8** ■ **Open 10am–8pm daily (for exhibitions)** ■ **www.kunsthalle-muc.de**

Built in 2001, the Kunsthalle buried deep within the glitzy Fünf Höfe shopping centre presents three to four high-profile exhibitions each year. Its themes range from Auguste Rodin and Walt Disney right through to the royal tombs of the Scythians.

A DAY IN THE NORTHERN OLD TOWN

▶ MORNING

Start at the **Frauenkirche** (see p89). After exploring the cathedral, make your way around the building to Albertgasse. At the end of this alley, you will reach Marienhof, which you should cross to get to **Dallmayr** (see p95). After visiting the delicatessen, go right and turn off Dienerstraße onto Hofgraben before turning right again onto Alter Hof. Take a left here onto Sparkassenstraße and just a few steps left again will get you to Münzstraße. The **Hofbräuhaus** at **Platzl** (see p89) will be on your left. Head north past Platzl to **Maximilianstraße** (see p93). After taking in the smart shops and boutiques on the way, you will pass the **Staatsoper** before arriving back at Theatinerstraße. A great place to stop for coffee and a snack is **Aran Fünf Höfe** (Theatinerstraße 12).

AFTERNOON

Once you've enjoyed a pit stop, explore the **Fünf Höfe** (see p93), or the Kunsthalle. Take the exit onto Kardinal-Faulhaber-Straße and turn right for **Salvatorkirche** (see p92) and **Literaturhaus** (see p92). Salvatorstraße then takes you back to Theatinerstraße once again. Keep left for **Odeons-platz** (see p12), where you will find the **Theatinerkirche** and **Feldherrnhalle**. Depending on the weather, you can spend the afternoon outside in the **Hofgarten** or at the **Residenz**. Once you've worked up an appetite, the **Spatenhaus an der Oper** (see p66) is the perfect place to round off the day in style.

The Best of the Rest

Market at Wittelsbacherplatz

Wittelsbacherplatz
MAP N2

Wittelsbacherplatz, the square just to the west of Odeonsplatz, is home to Ludwig Ferdinand's palace (now the headquarters of Siemens) and an equestrian statue of Maximilian I.

2 Max-Joseph-Platz
MAP N3

The Maximilian I Joseph memorial can be found in this early 19th-century square, which began with the construction of the Nationaltheater opera house. In summer, "Oper für alle" (Opera for all) streams the live performance on a giant screen.

3 Deutsches Theater-museum
MAP N2 ■ Galeriestraße 4a ■ Open 10am–4pm Tue–Sun ■ Adm ■ www.deutschestheatermuseum.de

This museum and library in the Hofgarten arcades showcases the history of German theatre.

4 Literaturhaus
MAP N3
■ Salvatorplatz 1
■ www.literaturhaus-muenchen.de

Located in a former Renaissance school, the Literaturhaus is used for literary gatherings and exhibitions. Brasserie OskarMaria (see p94) is on the ground floor.

5 Palais Porcia
MAP N3 ■ Kardinal-Faulhaber-Straße 12

The Rococo façade of this 1693 palace was designed by François de Cuvilliés the Elder.

6 Erzbischöfliches Palais
MAP N3 ■ Kardinal-Faulhaber-Straße 7

Formally the Palais Holnstein, the official residence of the archbishop is yet another creation of Cuvilliés the Elder, dating from 1737.

7 Münchner Kammerspiele

An Art Nouveau masterpiece, this theatre (see p55) has an exciting programme of plays, music and dance.

8 Promenadeplatz
MAP M3

In medieval times, this long, narrow square with its five memorials functioned as a salt market. The famous Hotel Bayerischer Hof and the Palais Montgelas now occupy its northern side.

9 Alte Münze
MAP N3 ■ Hofgraben 4

The Münzhof (mint) lies to the northeast of the Alter Hof. Dating from 1567, its three-storey arcaded courtyard was once home to stables, a library and an art chamber belonging to Albrecht V. The official state mint was established here in the 19th century.

10 Salvatorkirche
MAP M3
■ Salvatorstraße 17

Originally built in 1493–4, the Gothic cemetery church for the Frauenkirche has been a Greek Orthodox place of worship since 1829.

The Salvatorkirche

Shops

The *Sphere* at Fünf Höfe

Fünf Höfe
MAP N3 ■ www.fuenfhoefe.de

Brimming with restaurants and shops, this centre *(see p70)*, attracts seven million visitors every year.

2 Theatinerstraße and Residenzstraße
MAP N3

The shops on these streets *(see p70)* mainly appeal to fashionistas with refined tastes.

3 Maximilianstraße
MAP N3

Munich's most expensive shopping street *(see p70)*.

4 OBACHT'
MAP N4 ■ Ledererstraße 17

This shop on the corner of the Hofbräuhaus sells trinkets and curios with a local touch – perfect for souvenirs to take home.

5 Nymphenburger Porzellan
MAP N2 ■ Odeonsplatz 1

The flagship store of Porzellan Manufaktur Nymphenburg, located in the Nymphenburg Rotunda, is popular with lovers of design and porcelain alike.

6 Manufactum
MAP N3 ■ Dienerstraße 12

A fitting venue for this warehouse of self-proclaimed "good things", Manufactum is located in the historical grounds of the Alter Hof, the first Residenz.

7 Loden Frey
MAP N3 ■ Maffeistraße 5–7

While the traditional *dirndl* and *lederhosen* can be found in many places in Munich, the costumes here are of the highest quality.

8 Elly Seidl
MAP N3 ■ Maffeistraße 1

Locals can't get enough of the handmade pralines sold by this family-run company.

9 Team shops: FC Bayern and TSV 1860 München
MAP N3 ■ Orlandostraße 1 and 8

Football kits and all kinds of team memorabilia can be found in these two shops which are virtually opposite each other around the corner from the Hofbräuhaus.

Dallmayr's flagship store

10 Dallmayr
MAP N3 ■ Dienerstraße 14

The Marienhof branch of the former purveyor to the court has a top delicatessen and its own coffee blends. Its restaurant has two Michelin stars, and there's a lovely café bistro too.

See map on p88

Cafés and Bars

Visitors enjoying the outdoor seating at Brasserie OskarMaria

1 Brasserie OskarMaria
MAP N3 ■ Salvatorplatz 1

The café part of OskarMaria in the Literaturhaus serves its dishes on designer tableware (with quotes by Oskar Maria Graf). The gallery is a pretty spot, and outdoor seating is available in summer.

2 Café Kreutzkamm
MAP N3 ■ Maffeistraße 4

The home of the finest pralines and biscuits, this traditional café is the perfect spot in which to indulge.

3 Schumann's Tagesbar
**MAP N3 ■ Maffeistraße 6
■ Closed Sun**

This Fünf Höfe branch of the legendary Schumann's is a popular meeting place. Open during the day only.

4 Bar Centrale
MAP N4 ■ Lederer-straße 23 ■ (089) 223762

A stylish Italian retro bar (see p60) serving espressos in the morning and cocktails after sundown.

5 Pusser's
MAP N3 ■ Falkenturmstraße 9

Pusser's is a classic piano bar with a menu of over 200 cocktails.

Fruity cocktail

6 Tambosi
MAP F4 ■ Odeonsplatz 18

One of the oldest cafés in the city, Tambosi is a good place to enjoy a cup of coffee.

7 Café Luitpold
MAP N2 ■ Brienner Straße 11

Serving homemade pralines, cakes and daily specials, this former coffee house was rebuilt with its own palm garden after the war. It has a beautiful inner courtyard and a fabulous conservatory.

8 Alvino Bar
MAP N2 ■ Brienner Straße 10 ■ (089) 225004 ■ Closed Sun

Located near the Hofgarten, this fun spot (see p60) is one of the city's best bars.

9 Café Maelu
MAP N3 ■ Theatinerstraße 32

From macarons to tarts, this coffee shop in the Theatiner arcade offers a selection of mouth-watering confections.

10 Schumann's
MAP N2 ■ Odeonsplatz 6–7 ■ (089) 229060

Among the best places in the city for a drink, this Munich institution (see p61) has been in operation since 1982.

Restaurants

① Pageou
MAP N3 ■ Kardinal-Faulhaber-Straße 10 ■ (089) 2423 1310 ■ Closed Sun & Mon ■ www.pageou.de ■ €€€

The home *(see p64)* of Ali Güngörmüş and his Middle Eastern cuisine.

② Buffet Kull
MAP N4 ■ Marienstraße 4 ■ (089) 221509 ■ €€

Innovative Mediterranean cuisine is on the menu at this restaurant.

③ Pfälzer Residenz Weinstube
MAP N3 ■ Residenzstraße 1 ■ (089) 225628 ■ €

The Residenz *(see pp16–17)*, with six lounges, a wine cellar and outdoor seating, serves specialities such as Saumagen (sow's stomach), plus the best wines from the Palatinate region.

The world-famous Hofbräuhaus

④ Hofbräuhaus
■ €

Well known for its *Schweinshaxe* (ham hock) dishes, the Hofbräuhaus *(see p89)* also has good vegetarian options.

⑤ Südtiroler Stuben
MAP N3 ■ Am Platzl 8 ■ (089) 216 6900 ■ Closed Sun ■ www.schuhbeck.de ■ €€€

Enjoy gourmet fare at this restaurant *(see p65)* situated on the Alps.

PRICE CATEGORIES
Price of a three-course meal (or similar) for one, with a glass of wine or beer, including taxes and service.

€ below €30   €€ €30–60   €€€ over €60

⑥ Restaurant Alois
MAP N3 ■ Dienerstraße 14–15 ■ (089) 21350 ■ Closed Sun–Tue ■ €€€

Chef Diethard Urbansky serves spectacular six- and eight-course menus at this Michelin-starred restaurant *(see p65)* on the first floor of a traditional delicatessen.

⑦ Matsuhisa Munich
MAP N3 ■ Neuturmstraße 1 ■ (089) 2 9098 1875 ■ www.mandarinoriental.com ■ €€€

The only restaurant *(see p65)* in Germany headed by top chef Nobu Matsuhisa serves exquisite Japanese fusion cuisine.

⑧ Kulisse Theater-Restaurant
MAP N3 ■ Maximilianstraße 26 ■ (089) 294728 ■ €€

For over 50 years, the Kulisse restaurant at the Kammerspiele theatre has been serving fresh seasonal fare in a sophisticated atmosphere.

⑨ Restaurant Pfistermühle
MAP N3 ■ Pfisterstraße 4 ■ Closed Mon & Sun ■ www.pfistermuehle.de ■ €€€

The vault of this 16th-century former ducal mill offers the finest in Bavarian cuisine. Lunchtime express menu available for €20.

⑩ Azuki
MAP N3 ■ Hofgraben 9/Ecke Maximilianstraße ■ (089) 4132 7560 ■ €€

Located in a former post office with beautiful arcades, this restaurant serves Japanese and Vietnamese cuisine.

See map on p88 ←

🔟 Museum Quarter

The museum quarter (officially known as "Kunstareal München") is located in the Maxvorstadt district, bordering the university quarter. This is where you will find Bavaria's top art museums – the three Pinakotheken, Museum Brandhorst and the Egyptian Art Museum, among other world-class attractions.

The Glyptothek, Antikensammlungen and Lenbachhaus can also be found nearby, along with various smaller collections and a number of scientific museums, including the Paläontologisches Museum. With a selection of private galleries to boot, this area is definitely somewhere to spend a couple of days or more. There are plenty of cafés and bars where you can take a break in between museum visits. Alternatively, pack a picnic to enjoy in the parkland around the Pinakotheken.

Greek cup, Staatliche Antikensammlungen

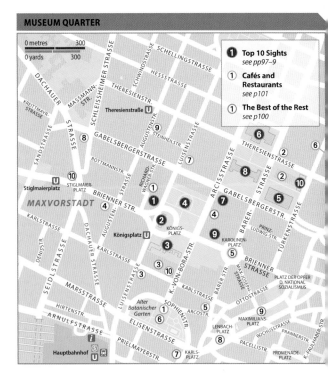

MUSEUM QUARTER

- **1** Top 10 Sights
  see pp97–9
- **1** Cafés and Restaurants
  see p101
- **1** The Best of the Rest
  see p100

Städtische Galerie im Lenbachhaus

① Städtische Galerie im Lenbachhaus

MAP L2 ▪ Luisenstraße 33 ▪ (089) 2339 6933 ▪ Open 10am–6pm Tue–Sun (until 8pm Thu) ▪ Adm ▪ www.lenbachhaus.de

Franz von Lenbach's villa (1887–91) has its own living quarters, studio wing, a further wing extension and a historic garden. A shining brass cube was added during extensive renovations completed in 2013. Thanks to a world-first combination of daylight and LEDs, the famous Blue Rider collection and other works can be seen in a new light. Both the exhibition space on the U-Bahn mezzanine and Café Ella belong to the museum.

② Königsplatz

MAP LM2

The city has Ludwig I to thank for this spacious square, with architect Leo von Klenze behind the Doric Propylaea and Ionian Glyptothek, which were built between 1816 and 1862. During the Nazi era, the square was paved and served as a parade ground. These days it is a green space and hosts outdoor events in the summer.

③ Staatliche Antikensammlungen

MAP LM2 ▪ Königsplatz 1 ▪ (089) 2892 7502 ▪ Open 10am–5pm Tue–Sun (until 8pm Wed) ▪ Adm ▪ www.antike-am-koenigsplatz.mwn.de

This collection of antiquities includes Greek, Etruscan and Roman vases, and bronze, terracotta, glass and jewellery from the 3rd millennium BC to the 5th century AD.

④ Glyptothek

MAP M2 ▪ Königsplatz 3 ▪ (089) 2892 7502 ▪ Open 10am–5pm Tue–Sun (until 8pm Thu) ▪ Adm ▪ www.antike-am-koenigsplatz.mwn.de

Munich's oldest public museum is the only one in the world that focuses exclusively on antique sculptures. Its highlights include 2,500-year-old archaic figures, the bust of Augustus, and the spectacularly lascivious Barberini Faun. The café is located in Room VIII and also offers seating out in the tranquil courtyard.

Students in front of the Glyptothek

The façade of the Pinakothek der Moderne museum

5 Pinakothek der Moderne

This enormous building (see p20) was designed by Stephan Braunfels as a fitting temple to 20th- and 21st-century art and design. All of its rooms are grouped around a central rotunda. The café offers indoor and outdoor seating.

6 Neue Pinakothek

One of the three museums that form the Pinakotheken (see pp18–20), the Neue Pinakothek opened in 1981. It was constructed on the same site as its predecessor, which had been destroyed in World War II. Based on plans by Alexander von Brancas, the building offers exceptional lighting for its internal spaces, which are packed with world-class artworks. The Hunsinger restaurant here has outdoor tables on the terrace to enjoy the sunny days. The museum is undergoing extensive renovation and will be closed until 2025.

7 Staatliches Museum Ägyptischer Kunst

MAP M2 ■ Gabelsbergerstraße 35 ■ (089) 2892 7630 ■ Open 10am–8pm Tue, 10am–6pm Wed–Sun ■ Adm ■ www.smaek.de

The entrance to this museum on the site of the University of Television and Film Munich (HFF) is reminiscent of the entrance to a burial chamber in the Valley of the Kings, leading into underground halls around a sunken courtyard. The ramp to the exhibition space leads to a superb statue of the god Horus. Further highlights include a facial fragment of Akhenaten, the coffin mask of Queen Sitdjehutj, and a statue of High Priest Bakenkhonsu.

8 Alte Pinakothek

This elongated building (see pp18–19) designed by Leo von Klenze has spacious rooms illuminated by skylights along with smaller cabinets on its north side, making it a model for other museum buildings of the early 19th century. The Alte Pinakothek suffered heavy damage in World War II, but it had been successfully rebuilt by 1957, with missing parts of the façade replaced by new, unrendered brickwork rather than reconstructed. The green spaces feature a sculpture exhibition, while the English-themed Café Klenze pays homage to the building's architects and is a good place for a break between museums.

The Rubens room in Alte Pinakothek

9 NS-Dokumentations-zentrum

MAP M2 ■ Brienner Straße 34 ■ (089) 2336 7000 ■ Open 10am–7pm Tue–Sun ■ Adm ■ www.ns-dokuzentrum-muenchen.de

A place of education and remembrance, this documentation centre presents Munich's past as the "Capital of the Movement". Opened in 2015, this cuboid structure of exposed white concrete stands on a historic spot: it was once the site of the "Brown House", the national headquarters of the Nazi Party. The permanent exhibition, "München und der Nationalsozialismus" (Munich and National Socialism), includes photographs, documents, texts, film projections and media stations.

The colourful Museum Brandhorst

10 Museum Brandhorst

Opened in 2009, this museum occupies a purpose-built multi-coloured building by Berlin-based architects Sauerbruch Hutton. The polygonal area above the foyer was designed specially for Cy Twombly's famous *Lepanto* cycle. Dominating some of the space are more of Twombly's large canvasses, while Andy Warhol is represented by some of his Elvis works, among others. Damien Hirst's work makes an appearance, as do artists including Jeff Koons, Sigmar Polke, Alex Katz and Mike Kelley. The Horst Esskultur-Bar is situated in the foyer.

EXPLORING THE MUSEUM QUARTER

MORNING

A good breakfast at **Café Lotti** *(see p101)* on Schleißheimer Straße will set you up for the museum tour. Head down Gabelsbergerstraße until you reach a right turn onto Richard-Wagner-Straße and you'll soon be at your first highlight – **Lenbachhaus** *(see p97)*. Here, you have the choice of stopping to browse the collections or moving on to the next museum. If you decide to keep going, turn left onto **Königsplatz** *(see p97)*, where you'll find the **Glyptothek** *(see p97)* and **Antikensammlungen** *(see p97)*. Straight ahead takes you to the **NS-Dokumentations-zentrum**. Follow Brienner Straße until you reach Karolinenplatz and turn left onto Barer Straße to find yourself between the **Alte Pinakothek** and **Pinakothek der Moderne**. Make your way across the lawn in front of Pinakothek der Moderne and take in the colourful façade of **Museum Brandhorst**. Then, head around the museum building and treat yourself to an ice cream from **Ballabeni** *(Theresienstraße 46)*. For something more substantial, keep going until you reach **Tresznjewski** *(see p101)*.

AFTERNOON

Follow Theresienstraße, then turn left onto Barer Straße to reach the **Alte Pinakothek**. If you're interested in ancient Egypt, then take a left onto Arcisstraße and walk down to the **Staatliches Museum Ägyptischer Kunst**. From here, follow Arcisstraße across Katharina-von-Bora-Straße and see the day out at **Park Café** *(see p101)*.

See map on p96 ←

The Best of the Rest

Exhibits, Paläontologisches Museum

1 Paläontologisches Museum

MAP L2 ■ Richard-Wagner-Straße 10
■ Open 8am–4pm Mon–Thu, 8am–
2pm Fri ■ www.palmuc.org

Visitors to the Palaeontology Museum can expect to find prehistoric fossils, including dinosaurs, mammoths, sabre-toothed tigers and the Mühldorf prehistoric elephant.

2 Museum Reich der Kristalle

MAP M1–2 ■ Theresienstraße 41
■ Open 1–5pm Tue–Sun ■ Adm

This museum next to the Pinakothek der Moderne holds a collection of minerals, crystals, precious stones, meteorites and much more.

3 Basilika St Bonifaz

MAP L2 ■ Karlstraße 34

Dating back to 1850, this abbey is the final resting place of Ludwig I.

4 Hochschule für Musik und Theater

MAP M2 ■ Arcisstraße 12

In the former "Führerbau" (Führer's building), this university is Germany's oldest training centre for theatre and music students. It also holds concerts.

5 Karolinenplatz

MAP M2

A black obelisk to commemorate those who fell in Napoleon's Russian Campaign of 1812 stands in this square, along with Amerikahaus and the stock exchange.

6 Alter Botanischer Garten

This former botanical garden is now a park (see p46).

7 Justizpalast

MAP L2 ■ Prielmayerstraße 7

Built by Friedrich Thiersch in 1890–97, the Palace of Justice and its atrium dominate Karlsplatz/Stachus.

8 Lenbachplatz

MAP M3

This green square featuring the Wittelsbacherbrunnen, a classical fountain, is always busy with cars, trams and shoppers.

9 Maximiliansplatz

MAP M3

Some of Munich's most popular clubs are situated around this park-style square with its many memorials.

10 Löwenbräukeller

This historic building (see p69), dating back to 1883, has several rooms, a ceremonial hall and a large beer garden. The Triumphator barrel is tapped in March.

Löwenbräukeller – a traditional pub

Cafés and Restaurants

1 Park Café
MAP L3 ■ Sophienstraße 7
■ (089) 5161 7980 ■ €€

This café occupies the site of the 1854 Glaspalast exhibition hall before it burned down. Great beer garden.

PRICE CATEGORIES

Price of a three-course meal (or similar) for one, with a glass of wine or beer, including taxes and service.

€ below €30   €€ €30–60   €€€ over €60

Outdoor seating at Tresznjewski

2 Tresznjewski
MAP M1 ■ Theresienstraße 72
■ (089) 282349 ■ €

Breakfast, lunch and dinner are served both inside and out at this café. In the evenings it transforms into a cocktail bar.

3 Hans im Glück
MAP L2 ■ Luisenstraße 14
■ (089) 9993 7818 ■ €

This burger paradise has something for everyone from beef lovers to vegans, and is great for satisfying post-pub hunger cravings.

Hans im Glück

4 Hamburgerei
MAP M2 ■ Brienner Straße 49 ■ (089) 2009 2015 ■ €

The burgers at this joint are made with only the freshest ingredients. Crunchy salads and vegetarian and vegan options are also on offer.

5 Hoiz
MAP M2 ■ Karlstraße 10
■ (089) 2880 8809 ■ Closed Sun ■ €€

This cosy brasserie offers a small selection of high quality dishes at reasonable prices.

6 Katzentempel München
MAP N1 ■ Türkenstraße 29
■ www.katzentempel.de ■ €€

A modern interior, a menu of vegan food and several resident cats are the main attractions at this friendly lunch spot near the Brandhorst.

7 Benko Café
MAP M1 ■ Luisenstraße 41
■ (089) 1276 5804 ■ €

A favourite with students, this café near the Glyptothek serves a menu of pastas, sandwiches and coffees.

8 Café Lotti
MAP L1 ■ Schleißheimer Straße 13 ■ (089) 6151 9197 ■ €

This pink, parlour-style café serves breakfast and light bites.

9 Café Jasmin
MAP L1 ■ Steinheilstraße 20 ■ (089) 4522 7406 ■ €

Furniture from the 1950s, panoramic wallpaper and ruffled curtains set the scene for a range of (often organic) breakfast, lunch and cake options.

10 Baalbek
MAP M2 ■ Karlstraße 27
■ www.restaurant-baalbek.de ■ €€€

Homemade-style Lebanese food is the speciality of this popular restaurant. There is also outdoor seating on the lovely terrace.

See map on p96

TOP 10 Schwabing and the University Quarter

At the beginning of the 19th century, the expansion of the old town to the north and west of Odeonsplatz began with the development of Maxvorstadt, which is home to the university quarter, including Ludwig-Maximilians-Universität and parts of the Technische Universität. Neighbouring Schwabing was a separate village in its own right until it was incorporated into Munich in 1890, and became a well-known alternative district, inhabited by artists and intellectuals. The Siegestor, a victory arch, is generally considered the entrance to Schwabing, although the "Schwabing vibe" extends as far as the fashionable Maxvorstadt quarter.

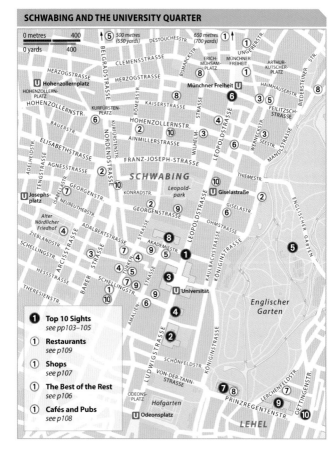

SCHWABING AND THE UNIVERSITY QUARTER

1	**Top 10 Sights** see pp103–105
1	**Restaurants** see p109
1	**Shops** see p107
1	**The Best of the Rest** see p106
1	**Cafés and Pubs** see p108

Siegestor, Munich's triumphal arch, at night

1 Ludwigstraße and Siegestor
MAP N1

After the old town wall was pulled down in 1800, Ludwig I commissioned a monumental boulevard in Italian Renaissance style. This "Italian mile" is bounded by the Feldherrnhalle *(see pp90–91)* to the south and Siegestor to the north. Modelled on the Arch of Constantine in Rome, the Siegestor is crowned by the figure of Bavaria riding a chariot drawn by four lions. Designed for victory parades honouring the Bavarian army, the gate was inscribed after the war with lines that translate as "Dedicated to victory, destroyed in war, an entreaty for peace".

2 Bayerische Staatsbibliothek
MAP N2 ■ Ludwigstraße 16 ■ www.bsb-muenchen.de

This major research library, which holds over 10 million books and 130,000 manuscripts, dates back to the 16th-century and incorporates the collections of Albrecht V and Wilhelm V. The present building was built by Friedrich von Gärtner in the style of a Renaissance palace.

3 Ludwig-Maximilians-Universität
MAP N1 ■ Geschwister-Scholl-Platz ■ www.uni-muenchen.de

In 1826 Ludwig I moved the university founded in 1472 in Ingolstadt to Munich. Its main assembly hall looks out onto Geschwister-Scholl-Platz and is surrounded by a number of faculty buildings.

4 Ludwigskirche
MAP N1 ■ Ludwigstraße 20

The Italian Romanesque-style university church, built between 1829 and 1843, is close to the Staatsbibliothek. King Ludwig I commissioned Friedrich von Gärtner to build the church that bears the monarch's name, on his monumental new boulevard, Ludwigstraße. The *Judgment Day* altar fresco by Peter Cornelius is the second-largest altar fresco in the world.

Ludwigskirche with its twin towers

Chinesischer Turm, Englischer Garten

5 Englischer Garten and Chinesischer Turm

Schwabing's "back garden" is a recreational paradise *(see pp22–3)*. The side streets to the right of Ludwigstraße and Leopoldstraße lead to two popular beer gardens: the Chinesischer Turm and Seehaus on Kleinhesseloher See.

6 Leopoldstraße and Münchner Freiheit

MAP G1–G3

Passing beneath the Siegestor, you enter Schwabing and the district's principal promenade: Leopoldstraße. Flanked by shops, street-side cafés and fast-food outlets, the boulevard has lost some of its 1960s and 1970s atmosphere – the time when a new generation of film-makers, students and artists were setting the tone – but there are still some interesting pockets. One of the street's highlights is the *Walking Man* (1995), a 17-m (55-ft) high sculpture by Jonathan Borofsky in front of house No. 36. At the northern end of Münchner Freiheit, in a café of the same name, tables are set out in summer beneath a larger-than-life statue of actor Helmut Fischer, star of German TV series *Monaco Franze – Der ewige Stenz* ("The Eternal Dandy"). Art Nouveau houses can be found on side streets off Leopoldstraße, notably

ART NOUVEAU

Munich is the birthplace of Jugendstil, the German version of Art Nouveau. In 1896, the first issue of the art journal *Jugend* (Youth) was published here, giving the new movement – characterized by its decorative, floral and linear style – its name. As early as 1892, over 100 artists had joined forces against the "tyranny" of Franz von Lenbach to form the Munich Secession.

Georgen-straße (No. 8–10) and Ainmiller-straße (No. 20, 22, 33, 34, 35 and 37). Take a detour onto Kaiserstraße for a glimpse of a pretty ensemble from the mid-19th century (Gründerzeit), or head to Hohenzollernstraße for a host of boutiques and shops. The other end of Leopoldstraße leads to the Englischer Garten.

7 Haus der Kunst

MAP P2 ■ Prinzregentenstraße 1 ■ (089) 2112 7113 ■ Open 10am–8pm Wed–Mon (until 10pm Thu) ■ Adm ■ www.hausderkunst.de

The Nazi past of the "House of German Art", dating from 1937, is documented in a free exhibition in the entrance area. The Haus der Kunst is a non-collecting art museum that presents around eight international contemporary art exhibitions every year.

Colonnade at the Haus der Kunst

8 Akademie der Bildenden Künste

MAP N1 ▪ Akademiestraße 2–4
▪ www.adbk.de

The Academy of Fine Arts, set in a Neo-Renaissance style building constructed between 1808 and 1886, has had an eventful history. The list of students who attended around 1900 reads like a who's who of modern art, including the likes of Kandinsky and Klee. An exhibition gallery is located on site.

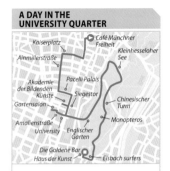

Bayerisches Nationalmuseum

9 Bayerisches Nationalmuseum

MAP P2 ▪ Prinzregentenstraße 3
▪ (089) 211 2401 ▪ Open 10am–5pm Tue–Sun (until 8pm Thu)
▪ Adm ▪ www.bayerisches-nationalmuseum.de

Packed with exhibits spanning two millennia, this museum offers a journey through the history of European art and culture. The building, dating from 1855, is almost as impressive as the exhibits, and worth the price of admission alone.

10 Sammlung Schack

MAP Q3 ▪ Prinzregentenstraße 9 ▪ Open 10am–6pm Wed–Sun ▪ Adm

This collection features around 180 masterpieces of 19th-century German art, mostly landscapes and historical scenes, plus legends and mythology.

A DAY IN THE UNIVERSITY QUARTER

Kaiserplatz
Café Münchner Freiheit
Kleinhesseloher See
Ainmillerstraße
Akademie der Bildenden Künste
Pacelli Palais
Gartensalon
Siegestor
Chinesischer Turm
Amalienstraße
University
Englischer Garten
Monopteros
Die Goldene Bar
Haus der Kunst
Eisbach surfers

► MORNING

Begin your day at the **Café Münchner Freiheit** (see p108). Later, stroll down Leopoldstraße and turn onto Kaiserstraße with its pretty houses (Lenin once lived at No. 46). Once you reach **Kaiserplatz** (see p106), follow Friedrichstraße to the corner of **Ainmillerstraße** with its Jugendstil houses (nos. 20–37). Continue on Friedrichstraße until you reach Georgenstraße. At no. 8 is the **Pacelli Palais** (see p106), next to the Palais Bissing. From here, return to Leopoldstraße and the **Akademie der Bildenden Künste** near the **Siegestor** (see p103). Walk to the **University** and cross the inner courtyard of the main building, which will bring you to the student district around Amalienstraße, with its many cafés and restaurants. If you're ready for a break, give **Gartensalon** (Türkenstraße 90) a try.

AFTERNOON

After taking a break, head to the **Englischer Garten**. Amble along to the **Kleinhesseloher See** (see p22) and take in the atmosphere. Make your way towards the beer garden at the **Chinesischer Turm** before climbing up to **Monopteros** (see p22), where the view of the city is simply magnificent. Next up, it's time to check out the **Eisbach surfers** (see p22) and then explore an exhibition at the **Haus der Kunst**. See out the evening in style with a cocktail at **Die Goldene Bar** (see p108) to the northeast.

See map on p102

The Best of the Rest

Interior of the Erlöserkirche

 Erlöserkirche
MAP G2 ■ Germaniastraße 4
This Protestant Art Nouveau church (1899–1901) occupies the northern end of Münchner Freiheit.

2 Elisabethplatz
MAP F3 ■ Market: Mon–Sat
A piece of old Schwabing, this square is named after the Austrian empress Sisi (short for Elisabeth). A market has been held here since 1903.

3 Wedekindplatz
MAP G2
Renovated in 2014, this square was once the heart of rural Schwabing. In 1962, it was the site of the local riots *(see p41)*, known as the "Schwabinger Krawalle".

 Alter Nordfriedhof
MAP F3 ■ Between Zieblandstraße, Arcisstraße, Adalbertstraße and Luisenstraße
There's nothing morbid about this former cemetery dating back to 1866. It is now a place of recreation and relaxation, and children love to play hide and seek among the old tombstones.

 Luitpoldpark
MAP F1
This park was created out of rubble from World War II. The restaurant in Bamberger House features ornate guest rooms and a beautiful terrace.

6 Nikolaiplatz & Seidlvilla
MAP G3 ■ www.seidlvilla.de
The Seidlvilla on Nikolaiplatz was saved from demolition and is now a centre for culture and community.

7 Archäologische Staatssammlung
MAP P2 ■ Lerchenfeldstraße 2
■ Closed for renovation until 2024
A collection of ancient and prehistoric discoveries from Bavaria.

8 Kaiserplatz and Kaiserstraße
MAP F2
The silhouette of St Ursula's church on Kaiserplatz has been immortalised by Kandinsky. Kaiserstraße is flanked with ornate buildings from the Gründerzeit.

9 Palais Pacelli
MAP F3 ■ Georgenstraße 8
This listed palace is a Neo Baroque-style residential building.

Borofsky's *Walking Man*

10 Walking Man
MAP F3
■ Leopoldstraße 36
Jonathan Borofsky's dynamic 17 m (56 ft) sculpture was commissioned by the Munich Re insurance group.

Shops

 Breitengrad
MAP N1 ▪ Schellingstraße 29

This shop offers cups and mugs, jewellery, a limited selection of clothing, and bags, not to mention various interesting goodies, such as gold sparklers.

 Living Colour
MAP F2
▪ Hohenzollernstraße 39

Clothes, pretty bags, cups, mugs, make-up bags and more – all featuring pretty, vibrant designs.

Quirky products at Living Colour

3 **Apartment**
MAP M1 ▪ Barer Straße 49

Yet another shop offering all kinds of colourful products, including tableware, gifts, and countless whimsical bits and pieces for kids of all ages.

4 **Lehmkuhl**
MAP G2
▪ Leopoldstraße 45

This fine bookshop on Leopoldstraße was founded in 1903 before being taken over by Fritz Lehmkuhl in 1913. It has a distinguished inventory and holds regular author readings.

5 **Amsel**
MAP F3 ▪ Adalbertstraße 14
▪ www.amsel-fashion.com

Find traditional Bavarian clothes, such as dirndls, jackets and vests, made to the highest possible quality and with serious attention to detail. The store provides great service.

6 **Biervana**
MAP F2
▪ Hohenzollernstraße 61

Beer, ale and craft beer – this shop offers over 600 different types with a particular focus on craft beers. It also stocks speciality beers.

7 **Picknweight**
MAP N1
▪ Schellingstraße 24

Vintage by the kilo: this shop is brimming with second-hand clothes that you pay for by weight. Another branch can be found on Tal.

8 **Autorenbuchhandlung**
MAP F2
▪ Wilhelmstraße 41

As the name suggests ("Authors' Bookshop"), this bookshop was founded 40 years ago by authors who wanted to free themselves from the book industry. Many author readings are held here.

9 **Words' Worth Books**
MAP F3 ▪ Schellingstraße 3
▪ www.wordsworth.de

If you forgot your holiday reading, this been-here-forever, English-language bookshop is the place to visit.

10 **Dear Goods**
MAP F3
▪ Friedrichstraße 28

This shop stocks only fair-trade, eco-friendly and vegan clothing, shoes and accessories.

Eco-friendly clothing at Dear Goods

See map on p102

Cafés and Pubs

1 Café Münchner Freiheit
MAP G2 ■ Münchner Freiheit 20

This long-established multilevel café with a large outdoor seating area has a larger-than-life sculpture of German actor Helmut Fischer, which overlooks the tables.

Café Münchner Freiheit

2 Café Reitschule
MAP G3 ■ Königinstraße 34

Located at the edge of the Englischer Garten, this traditional café features three patios, a beer garden and a conservatory. From the inside, patrons can see into the riding school. Champagne happy hour runs from 5 to 6:30pm.

3 Cotidiano
MAP F2 ■ Hohenzollern-straße 11

The breakfast menu at this branch of Gärtnerplatz's cult café offers something for everyone, including delicious goods from the in-house bakery. It also serves light bites in the afternoon and evening. Outdoor tables are available.

4 Gartensalon
MAP N1 ■ Türkenstraße 90 ■ Closed Mon

Tucked away in an inner courtyard on the Amalienpassage, this café is colourful and kitsch, with rainbow furniture and photo-covered walls. The garden is also a floral paradise. Breakfasts here are particularly good. Cards not accepted.

5 Zeitgeist
MAP N1 ■ Türkenstraße 74

Located close to the University, this well-established café serves amazing breakfasts and coffee.

6 Atzinger
MAP N1 ■ Schellingstraße 9

This once-legendary student pub has been extensively modernized, but the prices remain reasonable.

7 Café Ignaz
MAP F3 ■ Georgenstraße 67

This place has been serving delicious organic vegetarian and vegan goodies for over 30 years. It also has its own in-house bakery.

8 Die Goldene Bar
MAP P2 ■ Prinzregentenstraße 1

Located within the Haus der Kunst, this bar takes its name from its golden walls. Enjoy light meals here in the afternoon or stay until evening for cocktails mixed by Klaus St Rainer, former bartender of the year. Outdoor seating is available.

9 Schall & Rauch
MAP N1 ■ Schellingstraße 22

Small, cosy pub, serving local pasta dishes in a friendly atmosphere. Often packed to the rafters.

10 Café Katzentempel
MAP N1 ■ Türkenstraße 29

This vegetarian café is also home to six rescued cats, so you can enjoy a coffee with feline company.

The relaxed Café Katzentempel

Restaurants

Vivid dining room decor at Tantris

1 Tantris
MAP G2 ▪ Johann-Fichte-Straße
7 ▪ (089) 361 9590 ▪ Open noon–3pm
& 6:30pm–1am Wed–Sat ▪ €€€
This two-Michelin-starred restaurant
is Munich's finest for haute cuisine.

2 Georgenhof
MAP F3 ▪ Friedrichstraße 1
▪ (089) 3407 7691 ▪ €€
An Art Nouveau-style restaurant
with beer garden. Be sure to try
the pork dishes *Schweinebraten
(see p62)* or *Schweinshaxe*.

**3 Werneckhof Sigi
Schelling**
MAP G3 ▪ Werneckstraße 11
▪ Open noon–4pm & 6:30pm–
midnight Wed–Sat ▪ www.
werneckhof-schelling.de ▪ €€€
A fine-dining restaurant opened in
2021 with three to five course menus.
The dress code here is smart casual.

4 Ruff's Burger
MAP N1 ▪ Türkenstraße 63
▪ www.ruffsburger.de ▪ €
Locals love the homemade burgers
served here. Ruff's Burger also has
six other branches around the city.

5 Occam Deli
MAP G2 ▪ Feilitzschstraße 15
▪ €
Delicatessen with New York style
snacks and light dishes.

6 Arabesk
MAP P2 ▪ Kaulbachstraße 86
▪ (089) 333738 ▪ Closed L Sat &
Sun ▪ €€
Customers have been enjoying the
flavours of the Middle East followed
by shisha here for over 30 years.
The Lebanese food is delicious.

7 Max-Emanuel-Brauerei
MAP N1 ▪ Adalbertstraße 33
▪ (089) 271 5158 ▪ €
Dating back to around 1800, this
tavern serves traditional Bavarian
dishes. Its annual white parties to
celebrate Carnival, or Fasching, are
legendary. Great beer garden with
shaded areas.

8 Osterwaldgarten
MAP G2 ▪ Keferstraße 12
▪ (089) 3840 5040 ▪ €€
This idyllic beer garden and restaurant
at the Englischer Garten serves
Bavarian specialities. It is very
popular so it is best to book ahead.

**9 Ristorante Pizzeria
Bei Mario**
MAP F3 ▪ Adalbertstraße 15
▪ www.ristorantebeimario.de ▪ €
An Italian restaurant offering
Neapolitan pizzas as well as pasta,
meat and fish dishes.

10 Anh-Thu
MAP F3 ▪ Kurfürstenstraße 31
▪ (089) 2737 4117 ▪ Closed Mon ▪ €€
This contemporary restaurant serves
high-end Vietnamese cuisine.

See map on p102 ←

🔟 Along the Isar

Four distinct neighbourhoods flank the right bank of the Isar river: Giesing, Au, Haidhausen and Bogenhausen. While Bogenhausen is studded with villas, Haidhausen is a hotspot for nightlife. To the west of the Isar, on the left bank, lie the Englischer Garten and Lehel, a highly sought-after residential area containing some beautiful historic buildings. Most of the city's sights and attractions are located to the east of the river, including the Jugendstil masterpiece of the Müller'sches Volksbad, the Maximilianeum and Villa Stuck. Of the two islands in the middle of the Isar, Museuminsel holds the Deutsches Museum, a definite highlight in this area.

Friedensengel

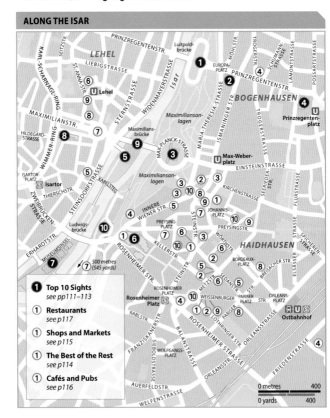

ALONG THE ISAR

1 Top 10 Sights
see pp111–113

1 Restaurants
see p117

1 Shops and Markets
see p115

1 The Best of the Rest
see p114

1 Cafés and Pubs
see p116

The grand façade of the Maximilianeum, seat of the Bavarian parliament

1 Friedensengel
MAP Q3 ■ Prinzregentenstraße

Soaring high above the banks of the Isar, the Friedensengel (Angel of Peace) of 1896–99 commemorates the Franco–Prussian war of 1870–71. Based on the Greek goddess Nike, this gilded figure stands 6 m (19.7 ft) tall. From its base, two sweeping flights of stairs lead down an escarpment to a terraced park with fountains.

2 Museum Villa Stuck
MAP Q3 ■ Prinzregentenstraße 60 ■ (089) 455 5510 ■ Open 11am–6pm Tue–Sun (until 10pm first Fri of month) ■ Adm ■ www.villastuck.de

Not far from the Friedensengel is the Villa Stuck – the *fin-de-siècle* masterpiece of painter Franz von Stuck. A miller's son, Stuck quickly rose to fame and was instrumental in the creation of the Munich Secession in 1892, which "discovered" Jugendstil (the local version of Art Nouveau). The villa has served as a museum since 1968. On view are private rooms, a permanent Art Nouveau collection, and changing exhibitions in the studio wing.

3 Maximilianeum
MAP Q4 ■ Max-Planck-Straße 1

Built by Friedrich Bürklein high on the banks of the Isar river, the Maximilianeum stands at the end of Maximilianstraße. Maximilian II commissioned this massive structure as a school for gifted students from poor backgrounds. Though the building has been the home of the Bavarian parliament since 1949, a school still occupies its rear; nowadays it accepts students with the highest grades.

4 Prinzregententheater
MAP R3 ■ Prinzregentenplatz 12 ■ www.theaterakademie.de

This theatre (see p54) is one of several monumental buildings on this stretch of Prinzregentenstraße. The Bayerische Staatstheater perform here, along with other companies. It was headed up by August Everding, whose legacy to the city includes the Bayerische Theaterakademie, a training ground for young talent. Next door is Prinzregentenbad, a public bath, and gourmet food shop Feinkost Käfer (see p115), is just across the street.

The Prinzregententheater

5 Praterinsel and Alpines Museum

MAP P4 ▪ Praterinsel 5 ▪ (089) 211 2240 ▪ Closed for renovation until 2023 ▪ Adm ▪ www.alpenverein.de

Located at the southern end of the Praterinsel, an island in the Isar, the Alpines Museum (see p45) documents the history of mountaineering and features special exhibitions throughout the year. An educational garden showcases the various types of rock found in alpine regions, while exhibitions and events are held in the halls of the former Riemerschmid distillery located at the northern end of the island. Tango dancers gather in the courtyard on summer evenings.

6 Gasteig

MAP P5 ▪ Rosenheimer Straße 5 ▪ www.gasteig.de

The site of the former Bürgerspital hospital and Bürgerbräukeller was transformed into the Gasteig cultural centre between 1978 and 1985, and its tiled bunker design was controversial. It is home to the Munich Philharmonic, the Carl-Orff concert hall and the state library. While the building is being renovated (due to end in 2027), concerts will take place in the Gasteig HP8 (see p54).

Kachina, Museum Fünf Kontinente

Exterior of the Gasteig

Transport at the Deutsches Museum

7 Deutsches Museum

Directly southwest from the Müller'sches Volksbad is the Deutsches Museum (see pp26–9), the largest museum of science and technology in the world.

8 Museum Fünf Kontinente

MAP P3 ▪ Maximilianstraße 42 ▪ (089) 2 1013 6100 ▪ Open 9:30am–5:30pm Tue–Sun ▪ Adm (free for under-18s) ▪ www.museum-fuenf-kontinente.de

This Neo-Renaissance building dates back to 1859–65 and was originally conceived for the Bayerisches National museum. The ethnological museum made this its home in 1926 and it features over 160,000 exhibits on the culture of non-European nations, with a collection on Bavarian rulers dating back more than 500 years. The museum café, max2, serves food in the arcades of Maximilanstraße.

9 The Isar Bridges

MAP P3

The Maximiliansbrücke is actually made up of two distinct bridges: the outer bridge leads to the Maximilianeum, while the inner

HAIDHAUSEN

This area used to lie beyond the city boundaries. A poor, rural village, it was referred to as a Glasscherbenviertel or "broken glass district", and some of the renovated inns are still reminiscent of this period. After 1871, French reparation payments launched development in this area, which explains the French names of the streets here.

bridge connects the west bank of the Isar with the Praterinsel. Ludwigsbrücke is another historically important bridge. Henry the Lion ordered that the original Isarbrücke (built in 1157–58 by the Bishop of Freising) be demolished to make way for a new bridge further to the south, which is where the Ludwigsbrücke is located today. All of the Isar bridges offer lovely views up and down the slow-moving river.

Müller'sches Volksbad on the Isar

⑩ Müller'sches Volksbad

MAP P4 ■ Rosenheimer Straße 1 ■ Open 7:30am–11pm daily ■ Adm ■ www.swm.de

Named for Karl Müller, the Munich citizen who financed the project, this Jugendstil bathing temple was built in 1897–1901, based on a design by Carl Hocheder. It was the first public pool in the city and remains one of the most beautiful. It is worth going for a swim just to admire the interior or enjoy the facilities, which include a steam room, though you can visit its stylish café without going for a dip.

A DAY ON THE ISAR

▶ MORNING

Setting off from **Müller'sches Volksbad** after coffee or breakfast at the in-house café, turn left out of the baths along the Isar to the footbridge, which leads to Praterinsel. Walk through the garden of the **Alpines Museum** and then across the island to **Maximiliansbrücke**, which will take you to the **Maximilianeum**. Make your way past the building in a semicircle and turn right onto Sckellstraße, which leads to **Wiener Platz** (see p114), with its market stalls and the Hofbräukeller. The narrow **An der Kreppe** (see p114) lane runs from this square to the historic inns in the "Glasscherbenviertel". The beer garden at the **Hofbräukeller** (see p114) is a great place to stop for a break.

AFTERNOON

After lunch, return to Sckellstraße, cross Max-Planck-Straße and head along Maria-Theresia-Straße, which is flanked by beautiful houses from the mid-19th-century/Jugendstil period. On the left-hand side of the street, the **Maximiliansanlagen** is a perfect park for a spot of ambling. Regardless of the route you take, all paths will eventually lead you to the **Friedensengel** (see p111). Continue along until you reach the Jugendstil **Museum Villa Stuck** (see p111). After a tour of the museum, make your way to **Feinkost Käfer** (see p115) on Prinzregentenstraße, a treat whether you opt for the deli bistro or the Käfer-Schänke fine-dining restaurant.

See map on p110 ⭠

The Best of the Rest

Johanniskirche's striking tower

1 Johanniskirche
MAP Q4 ■ Johannisplatz

This Neo-Gothic church has a truly striking 90-m- (295-ft-) high tower.

2 An der Kreppe
MAP Q4

Restored inns, originally designed for brick workers, give this corner of Haidhausen a village-like character.

3 Wiener Platz and Hofbräukeller
MAP Q4

At the heart of Haidhausen, Wiener Platz has hosted a market since 1889, while the Hofbräukeller (see p66) has been here since 1892.

4 Werksviertel
MAP R6

A former industrial area has been transformed into a cultural centre and nightlife hot spot.

5 St Lukas
MAP P4 ■ Mariannenplatz 3

St Luke's, in Lehel, built in 1893–96, is renowned for its choral concerts.

6 Pfarrkirche St Anna

A Neo-Romanesque parish church, St Anna (see p43) is the result of an architecture competition.

7 Maxmonument and Upper Maximilianstraße
MAP P3

The stretch of Maximilianstraße from the Altstadtring is flanked by ornate public buildings. A monument to Maximilian II (the Maxmonument) stands at the centre of a roundabout.

8 Regierung von Oberbayern
MAP P3 ■ Maximilianstraße 39

Maximilian II commissioned this Neo-Gothic building, which today serves as the seat of government for Upper Bavaria.

9 Lehel
MAP P3–4

Lehel is widely considered to be one of the city's most beautiful districts. A stroll in the area, especially in the vicinity of the Maxmonument, takes you past some stunning architecture.

10 Weißenburger Platz
MAP Q5

With the Glaspalastbrunnen, a tiered fountain at its centre, this square is the hub of the French quarter. An atmospheric Christmas market is held here every December.

The fountain in Weißenburger Platz

Shops and Markets

1 Ypnotic
MAP Q5 ■ Weißenburger Str. 12

Established more than 30 years ago, this independent shop stocks brightly coloured accessories and clothing with unusual designs. Designer labels such as Daily's, Freequent, Malvin and Anonyme can be found here.

2 Weltladen München
MAP Q5 ■ Weißenburger Straße 14

From organic coffee to handmade paper from India, this shop sells all sorts of fair trade products from around the world.

Livingroom shop and café

3 Livingroom
MAP Q4 ■ Wiener Platz 2

Vintage furniture and accessories for the kitchen, bathroom and living room. There is also a café.

4 Feinkost Käfer
MAP R3
■ Prinzregentenstraße 73

Catering king Gerd Käfer's Bogenhausen delicatessen is the place where celebrities come to do their food shopping.

5 Doppler Shop
MAP Q5
■ Metzstraße 15 (entrance on Sedanstraße)

This is the place for quirky and unique homeware, from stationery through to tableware and cushions.

Cute trinkets on sale in Kokolores

6 Kokolores
MAP Q5 ■ Wörthstraße 8

A shop full of interesting finds, from novelty postcards and stationery through to extra-special gifts.

7 The Lovely Concept
MAP G5 ■ Steinstraße 27

A modern store selling quirky clothing and accessories plus a variety of interior decor items.

8 Mohrmann Basics
MAP Q4 ■ Innere Wiener Straße 50

Striking fashion that's anything but ordinary – this small shop attracts customers to Haidhausen from miles around. Mohrmann stocks a wide range of different labels.

9 Buch & Töne
MAP Q5 ■ Weißenburger Str. 14

A charming bookshop stocking a mix of new and second-hand books, along with with audio-books and a selection of CDs.

10 Markt am Wiener Platz
MAP Q4

The permanent market stalls at Wiener Platz are open on weekdays and sell exquisite foodstuffs, from Alpine cheeses to Greek olives. It's a lovely place to stop for a coffee too.

Cushion at the Doppler Shop

See map on p110 ←

Cafés and Pubs

Maria Passagne bar in Munich

1 Maria Passagne
MAP Q5 ▪ Steinstraße 42
▪ (0177) 6924414 ▪ Closed Sun

The "living room" bar in this sushi restaurant is small and cosy. Booking is recommended, as the doorman stops letting anyone in once it's full.

2 Negroni
MAP Q5 ▪ Sedanstraße 9
▪ Closed Sun

Great cocktails are the order of the day at this American-style bar. The unpretentious menu features Italian-inspired cuisine.

3 Barroom
MAP Q5 ▪ Milchstraße 17
▪ Closed Sun & Mon

The smallest cocktail bar in Munich, this venue specializes in rum-based concoctions. Expect it to be busy.

4 Café la Maison
MAP Q5 ▪ Weißenburger Straße 6 ▪ Closed Mon

Laid-back, French café with a large cobbled terrace. Tasty vegan pastries and cakes are also available.

5 Café im Hinterhof
MAP Q5 ▪ Sedanstraße 29

This Art Nouveau-style café serves a generous breakfast. There's a quiet terrace in the inner courtyard.

6 Fortuna Cafebar
MAP Q5
▪ Sedanstraße 18

This small neighbourhood café with an Italian feel has tables both inside and out. It's an excellent place to come for Sunday brunch, and the hot chocolate is to die for.

7 Café Hüller
MAP N5 ▪ Eduard-Schmid-Straße 8 ▪ (089) 1893 8713

This neighbourhood café *(see p61)* is located in a pretty spot near the Isar river.

8 POLKA Bar
MAP Q5 ▪ Pariser Straße 38
▪ Closed Sun–Wed

Set in a basement vault, this bar is the perfect place to unwind and listen to music over a drink.

9 Johanniscafé
MAP Q4
▪ Johannisplatz 15

In a time-warped world of its own, the old-fashioned interior of this pub features a retro jukebox.

10 Lollo Rosso
MAP Q5 ▪ Milchstraße 1

The so-called Bar(varian) Grill serves up a combination of Mediterranean and Bavarian favourites, from steaks to snacks, and a long list of drinks.

Lollo Rosso Bar(varian) Grill interior

Restaurants

1 Chopan am Gasteig
MAP P5 ■ Rosenheimer Straße 8 ■ www.chopan-am-gasteig.de ■ €€

Munich has one of the largest Afghan communities in Europe, and this stylish restaurant is a good option to try traditional Afghan cuisine.

2 Nana
MAP Q5 ■ Metzstraße15 ■ www.nana-muenchen.de ■ €

Bringing a touch of Tel Aviv to Munich, Nana serves great mezzes.

3 Le Faubourg
MAP Q4 ■ Kirchenstraße 5 ■ (089) 475533 ■ Closed Mon & Sun ■ €€

Le Faubourg offers a bistro atmosphere complete with bijou tables and specials presented on a chalkboard, plus an excellent wine selection. A limited number of outdoor tables are available.

4 Rue des Halles
MAP Q4 ■ Steinstraße 18 ■ (089) 485675 ■ Closed Mon & Tue ■ €€

The oldest French restaurant *(see p65)* in Munich offers classic cooking at its finest.

Stone-baked pizza

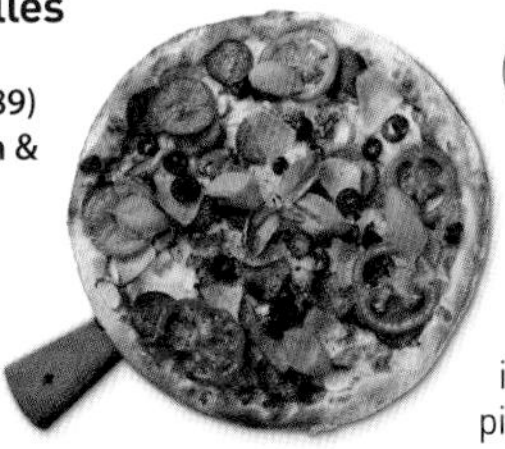

5 Bernard et Bernard
MAP Q4 ■ Innere Wienerstraße 32 ■ (089) 480 1173 ■ Closed L ■ €

What this crêperie lacks in size, it more than makes up for in quality, serving tasty crêpes, galettes and Breton-inspired dishes.

6 Vinaiolo
MAP Q5 ■ Steinstraße 42 ■ (089) 4895 0356 ■ Closed Sat L ■ www.vinaiolo.de ■ €€€

A Haidhausen favourite, this restaurant *(see p64)* has a shop-like dining space and Mediterranean dishes on the menu.

PRICE CATEGORIES

Price of a three-course meal (or similar) for one, with a glass of wine or beer, including taxes and service.

€ below €30   €€ €30–60   €€€ over €60

Seafood on display at Chez Fritz

7 Chez Fritz
MAP Q4 ■ Preysingstraße 20 ■ (089) 448 7676 ■ Closed L & Mon ■ €€

This brasserie offers an upscale French menu with a retro atmosphere. Tables available on Preysingplatz.

8 Il Cigno
MAP R5 ■ Wörthstraße 39 ■ (089) 448 5589 ■ Closed Sun ■ €

People in Munich enjoy Italian food, and Il Cigno is a great place to enjoy pizza and pasta. Outdoor seating is available if the weather is good.

9 Zum Kloster
MAP Q4 ■ Preysingstraße 77 ■ (089) 447 0564 ■ €

This rustic restaurant is the place to go for organic home cooking. Outdoor seating is available beneath cherry trees on a quiet street.

10 PreysingGarten
MAP Q4 ■ Preysingstraße 69 ■ (089) 688 6722 ■ €

Breakfast (until 3pm), lunch and dinner are served Italian style at this wood-panelled venue. It also has an attractive garden and play area.

See map on p110

TOP₁₀ South West

The area to the west and south of the old town is diverse and surprisingly green. Ludwigsvorstadt is the site of the huge Hauptbahnhof (main railway station) and Theresienwiese, the venue for the annual Oktoberfest. To the south of Sendlinger Tor and the Gärtnerplatz quarter, Isarvorstadt is home to a large number of shops and cafés, while the nearby Isar riverbanks offer a splendid backdrop. The Westend area, west of Theresienwiese, is a multicultural quarter that is undergoing rapid change, while the southwestern corner of this part of Munich is home to the green spaces of the Westpark.

**Statue of Bavaria,
Theresienhöhe**

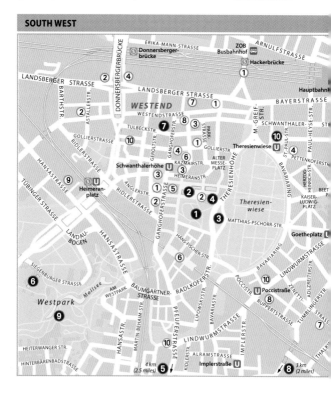

SOUTH WEST

1 Bavariapark
MAP J4–5

The park directly behind the Bavaria statue dates back to Ludwig I, who commissioned the creation of the "Theresienhain" (as it was then known) at the start of the 19th century. In 1872, the park was opened to the public and it later became an exhibition space when the Alte Messe events venue was established. Today, locals enjoy the park as somewhere to go jogging or to simply relax. It is home to a number of old stone sculptures as well as the Wirtshaus am Bavariapark (see p125).

2 Altes Messegelände and Verkehrszentrum
MAP J4 ■ Am Bavariapark 5

The site of the Alte Messe (Old Fair) around Bavariapark and Theresienhöhe has undergone

Vehicles at the Verkehrszentrum

massive development since the trade fair moved to Riem. Contemporary residences have been built on the former exhibition grounds, including the tower of the Steidle-Haus, and many of the former exhibition halls have now been converted for cultural use. The Verkehrszentrum (a branch of the Deutsches Museum), which showcases the history of transport, is housed here (see pp26–9) in three protected Art Nouveau halls. Its permanent exhibition divides its collection of vehicles into three themes: urban transport, travel, and technology.

3 Bavaria Statue and Theresienwiese
MAP D5 ■ Theresienhöhe 16 ■ Open Apr–mid-Oct: 9am–6pm daily (Oktoberfest: until 8pm) ■ Adm

Standing 18.5 m (61 ft) tall, the bronze statue of Bavaria towers over her surroundings and has an observation platform inside her head. Leo von Klenze's Ruhmeshalle (Hall of Fame), with busts honouring famous Bavarians, stands behind the colossal figure. Bavaria overlooks Theresienwiese, home of many events – most notably the Oktoberfest (see pp34–5). A festival was held here on 12 October 1810 to celebrate the wedding of crown prince Ludwig and Therese von Sachsen-Hildburghausen. In honour of the bride, the festival ground was named Theresienwiese.

0 metres   500
0 yards   500

4 Alte Kongresshalle
MAP J4 ■ Theresienhöhe 15

Built in 1952–3 in retro-futuristic style, the Old Congress Hall is one of a number of buildings that survived from the former exhibition grounds. Equipped with state-of-the-art technology, it often hosts cultural and social events. The hall's former teahouse is home to the Kongress Bar, while the Wirtshaus am Bavariapark (see p125) can be found at the south end of the site.

5 Tierpark Hellabrunn
MAP E7 ■ Tierparkstraße 30 ■ (089) 625080 ■ Open summer: 9am–6pm daily (winter: until 5pm) ■ Adm ■ www.hellabrunn.de

When Hellabrunn was founded in 1911, it was the first zoo in the world to arrange its 750 animals based on their geographic origins. Highlights include the jungle tent with its feline predators, a tropical forest and aquarium pavilion (where monkeys, snakes and fish inhabit a jungle and coral-reef habitat), the giraffe savannah and the ape enclosure.

A mascot in action at the Audi Dome

6 Audi Dome
MAP C6 ■ Grasweg 74 ■ Adm ■ www.fcb-basketball.de

The Rudi-Sedlmayer-Halle was built in 1972 as a basketball venue for the Olympic Games. It then hosted rock concerts, trade fairs and boxing events, and has been home to the Bayern Munich basketball club since becoming the Audi Dome in 2011.

7 Westend
MAP J3–4

The Westend area, which is officially known as Schwanthalerhöhe after sculptor Ludwig von Schwanthaler, developed with the start of industrialization. Schwanthaler designed the Bavaria statue, a masterpiece cast by Ferdinand von Miller from 1840 to 1850. This section of the city was long considered a "Glasscherbenviertel" (broken glass, or pub district) with a multicultural vibe, but is now a real mix of old and new. The relocation of the trade fair gave rise to the construction of new residential areas, although the neighbourhood still retains some original buildings. Traditional pubs and shops sit beside chic cafés and stylish boutiques. This area around the Hauptbahnhof is particularly lively due to its flourishing immigrant communities, who have opened up a variety of shops and cafés here.

Visitors at Tierpark Hellabrunn

8 **Flaucher**

MAP E6

This is Munich's best beach by the Isar. Every summer, sun worshippers flock to the gravel banks along the southern Isar, and many stop in at the pretty beer garden of the same name.

9 **Westpark**

MAP BC6

A smaller, Westend version of the Englischer Garten, Westpark was created for the fourth International Horticultural Exposition in 1983. Among its attractions are landscaped gardens, barbecue and picnic facilities, two large lakes, and two beer gardens. The Asian section with its Japanese garden and Thai *sala* (pavilion) is especially beautiful.

Thai pavilion at Westpark

10 **Paulskirche**

MAP K4 ■ St-Pauls-Platz 11

The view over the Wiesn (annual site of the Oktoberfest) from the 97-m (318-ft) high tower of this Neo-Gothic church is simply glorious, once you've climbed the 252 steps. St Paul's was the scene of tragic events in 1960, when a US military aircraft hit the tower and crashed down on a tram, shortly after take-off from Munich-Riem airport.

A DAY IN WESTEND

▶ **MORNING**

Begin at the **Bavaria** statue *(see p119)*. Climb up and enjoy the view across Theresienwiese. Behind the Ruhmeshalle is the **Bavariapark** *(see p119)*. Walk through to its northern end and visit the **Verkehrszentrum** *(see p119)*, a branch of the Deutsches Museum housed in three halls. Cross Heimeranstraße and follow the tree-lined passage to Kazmairstraße (check out the beautiful sgraffito at no. 21). Just a few houses further down on the left, you'll find **SchokoAlm** *(Kazmairstraße 33)*, which serves delicious coffee, cocoa, chocolates, gingerbread and cake. Next, stroll through the up-and-coming Westend quarter from **Gollierplatz** *(see p122)* to **Georg-Freundorfer-Platz** *(see p122)*. For lunch, try **Marais** *(see p123)* or **La Kaz** *(see p125)*.

AFTERNOON

Head back through Bavariapark, and across the Quartiersplatz Theresienhöhe (over the S-Bahn) to reach the eastern section of **Westpark**. Stroll westwards until you come to "Die Arche" by Steffen Schuster, with a whole host of colourful animals. Making your way past the turtles in the **Mollsee**, past the **Audi Dome** and over the bridge (Mittlerer Ring), you will soon reach the western section of the park, which is home to a Thai sala, Chinese and Japanese garden, rose garden and a lake complete with a stage for open-air performances. If you're ready for a beer and a snack, call in at the **Wirtshaus am Rosengarten** restaurant *(Westendstraße 305)*.

See map on pp118–19

The Best of the Rest

 Hackerbrücke
MAP K3

One of the few wrought-iron arch bridges in Germany, the Hacker-brücke crosses the tracks in front of the Hauptbahnhof (train station; also the site of the central bus terminal).

 Hauptzollamt
MAP C4 ▪ Landsberger Straße 124

The main customs office, with its Jugendstil elements and glass dome, dates back to 1912.

 Georg-Freundorfer-Platz
MAP J4

This square with a football pitch, summer curling and a climbing garden is a popular hangout.

4 **Central Tower**
MAP D4 ▪ Landsberger Straße 110

This distinctive, 23-storey building is one of Munich's few skyscrapers.

5 **Endlose Treppe**
MAP J4 ▪ Ganghoferstraße 29

Olafur Eliasson's *Endlose Treppe* (Endless Staircase) is located in the courtyard of the KPMG offices.

Endlose Treppe **by Olafur Eliasson**

Playground at the Quartiersplatz

6 **Quartiersplatz Theresienhöhe**
MAP J5

This concrete ceiling above the railway tracks was designed in 2010 as a landscape sculpture, complete with hills, dunes and a play area.

7 **Augustiner-Bräu**
MAP J3 ▪ Landsberger Straße 35

Munich's oldest brand of beer is brewed in the brickwork Augustiner brewery, which also has its own beer hall called the Augustiner Bräustuben *(see p125)*.

8 **Alter Südfriedhof**
MAP E6

Many prominent figures are buried at the city's oldest central cemetery. Today, local residents like to take a stroll under its ancient trees.

9 **ADAC Zentrale**
MAP C5 ▪ Hansastraße 19

This showstopper Westend building (93 m/305 ft tall) features over 1,000 windows that shimmer in 22 colours. It is home to ADAC, the German motoring organization.

10 **Gollierplatz**
MAP D5

This beautiful, tree-lined square at the heart of Westend features a number of Jugendstil houses and the Neo-Romanesque St Rupert's church.

Cafés and Pubs

(1) Lohner und Grobitsch
MAP D5 ▪ Sandtnerstraße 5

This former grocery shop is now a café that still retains some of its old charm. Good cakes, as well as breakfast and salads.

(2) Café Westend
MAP D5
▪ Ganghoferstraße 50

This combined café, bar and restaurant serves a great-value business lunch. It also has pool tables and bowling alleys in the basement.

(3) Marais
MAP J3 ▪ Parkstraße 2

A former shop with a nostalgic interior, including wooden chests and toy prams. Guests can drink coffee in the window display.

(4) Café am Beethovenplatz
MAP L4 ▪ Goethestraße 51

This traditional café, in a listed Belle Époque house belonging to the Hotel Mariandl, offers a real taste of Viennese coffee-house culture. There is live classical or jazz music every day and a small garden to enjoy in summer.

(5) Aroma Kaffeebar
MAP M5 ▪ Pestalozzistraße 24

This hipster café in a former pawn shop is located in the Glockenbach quarter. In addition to coffee and cakes, there is a selection of light meals available. The café also has its own shop, which stocks a real mishmash of fun products.

(6) München 72
MAP M5 ▪ Holzstraße 16
▪ Closed Mon

Named in memory of the attack at the 1972 Olympics, this café bar is brimming with 1970s furnishings – including a bicycle hanging behind the bar. Popular with mums in the afternoons, München 72 draws in a more varied crowd in the evening.

The long-running German TV crime show *Tatort* is screened here on Sundays.

Cocktail

(7) Tagträumer
MAP L6
▪ Dreimühlenstraße 17
▪ Closed Mon

This coffee shop in the Schlachthof quarter is steeped in history – it was previously a police station and a butcher's shop, to name just two of its former incarnations – and is an atmospheric place for breakfast.

(8) Substanz
MAP K6 ▪ Ruppertstraße 28

This long-established pub, bar and live club hosts famous bands and newcomers alike, not to mention monthly poetry slams. It's very popular, so arrive early to get a seat.

Bar and seating area at Ferdings

(9) Ferdings
MAP M5 ▪ Klenzestraße 43
▪ Closed Sun & Mon

Don't be put off by the bathrobes in the cloakroom – they are provided to keep smokers warm outside. This industrial bar serves regional tapas and a great selection of drinks.

(10) Café Mozart
MAP L4 ▪ Pettenkoferstraße 2

This café-restaurant with 1960s decor serves breakfast, as well as dinner and cocktails in the evening.

See map on pp118–19

Shops

1 Comic Dealer
MAP J4 ▪ Gollierstraße 16

A comic shop that also sells manga, T-shirts, posters, models and more.

2 WARE FREUDE
MAP C5 ▪ Westendstraße 142

Perfect for souvenir shopping, this place sells T-shirts, postcards and decorative items. The brand is synonymous with regional design and ecological production.

3 SchokoAlm
MAP J4 ▪ Kazmairstraße 33

When it comes to chocolate, this chocolatier offers everything you could dream of and more, including tempting truffles, sweets and pastries, and gorgeous cakes. It also has its own café with limited outdoor seating.

4 louloute
MAP J4 ▪ Gollierstraße 33

This shop offers sewing courses for beginners and pros alike. If you don't want to create your own design, you can buy items from loulute's collection.

Colourful trinkets on offer at Roly Poly

5 Roly Poly
MAP M5 ▪ Fraunhoferstraße 9

This designer fabric shop sells organic materials and accessories for both adults and kids. It also offers sewing courses. If you're interested in needlecraft, then Roly Poly is definitely worth a visit.

Shop window, Götterspeise

6 Götterspeise
MAP M5 ▪ Jahnstraße 30

The best hang-out for chocolate fans in the Glockenbach quarter, this shop offers a whole host of tasty treats, vegan and lactose-free goodies, and gifts. The café serves cakes, pastries and coffee.

7 Antonetty
MAP M5 ▪ Klenzestraße 56

Bags, clothes and a variety of other items made of leather are to be found in this shop. The little leather animals make good gifts.

8 Rocket
MAP N5 ▪ Reichenbach-straße 41

This shop stocks the latest streetwear, shoes, accessories, bags and jewellery for adults and children.

9 Wohnpalette
MAP M5 ▪ Fraunhoferstraße 13

If you're shopping for picture frames, metal signs, decorative lighting or candlesticks, then you need look no further than Wohnpalette.

10 ReSales
MAP K6 ▪ Lindwurmstraße 82

Located to the south of the Theresienwiese, this shop sells good-quality vintage and second-hand clothing.

Restaurants

1 Augustiner Bräustuben
MAP J3 ■ Landsberger
Straße 19 ■ (089) 507047 ■ €
A traditional Bavarian tavern at the
heart of the Augustiner brewery.

2 Wirtshaus am Bavariapark
MAP J4 ■ Theresienhöhe 15
■ (089) 4521 1691 ■ €
A great pub with a beer garden
(see p61) at the edge of Bavariapark.

3 Junge Römer
MAP M5 ■ Pestalozzistraße 23
■ Closed Mon ■ www.jungeroemer-
muenchen.de ■ €
An Italian restaurant with a large
selection of pasta and *pinsa*
(a type of pizza with less salt).

4 Speiselokal Lenz
MAP K4 ■ Pettenkoferstraße 48
■ (089) 5523 9771 ■ €
This restaurant near Theresienwiese
serves international food for lunch
and dinner. Outdoor seating available.

5 Paulaner Bräuhaus
MAP L6 ■ Kapuzinerplatz 5
■ (089) 544 6110 ■ €
This traditional brewery tavern has a
bar, lounge areas and a beer garden.

6 La Kaz
MAP J4 ■ Ligsalzstraße 38 ■ (089)
7699 0710 ■ Closed L, Mon–Fri ■ €
Customers at this popular,
independently owned pub perch

PRICE CATEGORIES
Price of a three-course meal (or similar)
for one with a glass of wine or beer,
including taxes and service.

€ below €30   €€ €30–60   €€€ over €60

on colourful stools at wooden
tables to enjoy well-chilled wines
and excellent food.

7 Wirtshaus im Schlachthof
MAP L6 ■ Zenettistraße 9
■ (089) 7201 8264 ■ Closed L &
Tue ■ €
This tavern with a beer garden
and stage hosts a range of events.

8 Zur Schwalbe
MAP J3 ■ Schwanthalerstraße
149 ■ (089) 2302 1447 ■ €€
Try dishes from the Alps here,
such as pretzel salad or mountain
cheese dumplings.

9 La Vecchia Masseria
MAP L4 ■ Mathildenstraße 3
■ (089) 550 9090 ■ €
Arguably the best Italian restaurant
in town, La Veccia serves traditional
dishes in a welcoming atmosphere.

10 Stemmerhof
MAP D6 ■ Plinganserstraße 6
■ (089) 7675 5965 ■ Closed Sun ■ €€
This urban yet rural place in a former
farmyard serves European favourites.

Industrial chic decor at La Kaz

See map on pp118–19

TOP 10 North West

West of Maxvorstadt, Munich's northwest includes the districts of Neuhausen and Nymphenburg. The Hirschgarten – Bavaria's largest beer garden and a must for lager connoisseurs – is located in the far west of this part of the city. The Olympiapark and its varied attractions are located to the north, rubbing shoulders with one of Munich's largest companies, BMW, whose museum and BMW Welt attractions lie close to the car-maker's state-of-the-art plant.

Peony bloom

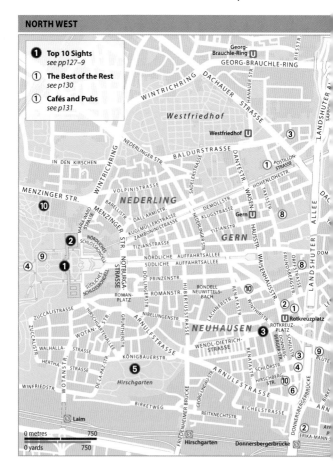

1 Schloss Nymphenburg

Originally built as the 17th-century summer palace of Elector Ferdinand and Adelaide of Savoy, but much expanded since, Schloss Nymphenburg is one of the best places to escape the bustle of the city centre. Once you've toured the palace's many rooms, spend some time in the magnificent landscaped gardens, which are dotted with pavilions. Nymphenburg is famous for its porcelain, and a factory shop is located just outside the Schloss entrance. There are also a couple of museums in the

Schloss Nymphenburg

palace wings that are worth a visit. There's also a café-restaurant *(see p130)* where you can refuel.

2 Museum Mensch und Natur

MAP B2 ■ (089) 179 5890 ■ Open 9am–5pm Tue–Fri, 10am–6pm Sat & Sun ■ Adm ■ www.mmn-muenchen. snsb.de

Located in a separate wing of the Schloss Nymphenburg, this museum guides you on a journey through biological, earth and life sciences, as you discover the history of Earth and life as we know it through dioramas, natural objects and interactive exhibits. One of the real stars of the exhibition is Bruno, the bear who wandered over the Alps into Bavaria from Italy in 2006 and was ultimately shot, despite protests.

3 Neuhausen
MAP C3

Rotkreuzplatz is the centre of Munich's second-largest urban district, with countless bars and restaurants lining the streets surrounding the square. The many old buildings make it a popular residential area, and the quality of life here is excellent thanks to the multitude of green spaces such as the Botanischer Garten, Schlosspark Nymphenburg and the Hirschgarten.

BMW Welt and the BMW Museum

4 BMW Welt

■ MAP E1 ■ Am Olympiapark 1 ■ (089) 1 2501 6001; EssZimmer: (089) 3 5899 1814 ■ Building: open 7:30am–midnight daily (from 9am Sun); exhibitions: open 9am–6pm ■ www.bmw-welt.com

This prestigious BMW building has been a prominent feature at Olympiapark since 2007. As the car manufacturer's distribution and experience centre, it has become one of the most popular attractions in Munich. Its distinctive double-cone design houses several exhibitions, as well as hosting political, art and cultural events. In addition to its many shops, you can find several restaurants here, including the Michelin-starred EssZimmer – home of top chef Bobby Bräuer.

5 Hirschgarten

■ MAP B3–4 ■ Hirschgarten 1 ■ (089) 1799 9119 ■ Open 10am–midnight (beer garden: from 11:30am) ■ www.hirschgarten.de

To the south of Schloss Nymphenburg, this beer garden is home to its own fallow deer enclosure, a nod to the park's former function as an electoral hunting ground (from 1780). A new hunting lodge was built in 1791 and became a popular destination for locals – particularly when it was licensed to sell beer. This was the first step in the venue becoming the tavern it is today, although it's probably best known for its huge beer garden (Bavaria's largest)

where customers enjoy Augustiner beer in the shade of the chestnut trees. The 40-ha (99-acre) park is a much-loved site for sport and relaxation, including playgrounds, hills for tobogganing, and barbecue pits.

6 Sea Life

This aquarium *(see p53)* can be found at the Olympiapark and is a popular destination for visitors of all ages. One of the highlights is the shark tunnel.

7 Olympiapark

Created in north Schwabing for the 1972 Summer Olympics, this site *(see pp32–3)* is the top sport and recreational ground in Munich.

8 BMW Museum

■ MAP E1 ■ Am Olympiapark 2 ■ Open 10am–6pm Tue–Sun ■ Adm ■ (089) 1 2501 6001 ■ www.bmw-welt.com

At the foot of the four-cylinder BMW Headquarters lies the bowl-shaped BMW Museum. This flat-roofed building is home to a permanent exhibition featuring over 120 cars,

Classic luxury car at the BMW Museum

motorbikes and engines spanning nine decades of BMW history, while the "bowl" hosts changing exhibits.

9 Circus Krone
MAP K2 ■ Zirkus-Krone-Straße 1–6 ■ Tickets: www.circus-krone.com

While the circus tours in the summer, the Circus Krone Building hosts concerts and other events. Circus season traditionally begins on Christmas Day and offers three different shows until the end of February.

Circus Krone's Christmas show

10 Botanischer Garten
MAP A2 ■ Menzinger Straße 65 ■ (089) 1786 1316 ■ Open Jan, Nov & Dec: 9am–4:30pm daily; Feb, Mar & Oct: until 5pm; Apr & Sep: until 6pm; May, Jun, Jul & Aug: until 7pm ■ Adm ■ www.botmuc.de

Around 14,000 plant species from across the globe are cultivated outdoors and in greenhouses in these botanical gardens, which were laid out at the start of the 20th century. Highlights here include the Alpinum and its alpine flora, the Arboretum with trees from around the world, June's spectacular rhododendron display, the fern glen, an insect pavilion full of butterflies and the greenhouses.

A DAY IN THE NORTH WEST

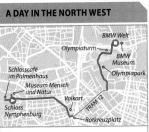

▶ MORNING

Start the day at **Schloss Nymphenburg** *(see p127)*. Depending on the weather, you can enjoy a relaxed stroll through the Schlosspark or else marvel at the palace interior. For a coffee break, head into the **Schlosscafé im Palmenhaus** *(see p130)*. Note that Nymphenburg is home to a couple of interesting museums, such as the **Museum Mensch und Natur** *(see p127)*. Once you're done here, wander down Auffahrtsallee towards Nymphenburger Straße and stop for lunch at the **Volkart** *(see p131)* tapas bar on Volkartstraße.

AFTERNOON

From Nymphenburger Straße, it isn't far to **Rotkreuzplatz**. From here, take tram 12 (towards Scheidplatz) as far as Infanteriestraße and head down Ackermannstraße. You'll reach the **Olympiapark** in no time, where you can marvel at the architecture of the Olympic buildings. Don't forget to take in the view from the **Olympiaturm** *(see p130)* – on a clear day you'll be able to see distant mountains. Once you've made your way back down to earth, there's plenty more exciting architecture to enjoy with **BMW Welt** waiting for you on the other side of the street. There's even the opportunity to make a quick detour to the **BMW Museum,** if you're interested. After a busy day's sightseeing, you can round things off at the exquisite EssZimmer restaurant at BMW Welt or the revolving restaurant at the top of the Olympiaturm.

See map on pp126–7

The Best of the Rest

Dantebad in the stadium

6 Olympiaturm
At 290 m (951 ft), the Olympic tower *(see pp32–3)* – and its view – are not to be missed.

7 Augustiner-Keller
MAP K2 ■ Arnulfstraße 52
This historic restaurant has a beer garden filled with old chestnut trees. Augustiner Edelstoff is served on tap.

1 Dantebad
MAP C2 ■ Postillonstraße 17 ■ Open summer: 9am–8pm daily; rest of year: until 6pm ■ www.swm.de
This open-air facility has more pools than any other swimming site in Munich. There's also a heated zone to enjoy in winter.

2 Freiheiz
MAP D4 ■ Rainer-Werner-Fassbinder-Platz 1
The renovated hall of this former thermal power station is a popular venue for concerts and events.

3 Borstei
MAP C1 ■ Dachauer Straße 140
A mini village within the city, this residential area was built in 1924–9 as an alternative to house sharing. It has courtyards, gardens, fountains and a museum.

4 Nymphenburger Kanal
MAP A3
Schloss Nympenburg's canal was commissioned by Max Emanuel in 1701. The section in front of the palace is a popular spot for curling when it freezes over in winter.

5 Utopia
MAP E3 ■ Heßstraße 132
These Neo-Romanesque former stables are now used to host events including theatre performances, concerts and the Opernfestspiele.

8 Taxisgarten
MAP C2 ■ Taxisstraße 12
Established in 1924, this beer garden hosts brass band performances on the weekend.

9 Schlosscafé im Palmenhaus
MAP A3 ■ Schloss Nymphenburg, entrance 43 ■ Open 11am–6pm daily ■ www.palmenhaus.de
A former greenhouse, this building is now a bright and airy café-restaurant with tables in the garden.

10 Herz-Jesu-Kirche
MAP C3 ■ Lachnerstraße 8
Built in the late 1990s, this church resembles a semi-transparent cube with a blue front. The interior features a free-standing wooden cube with slats that create different light effects.

The modern Herz-Jesu-Kirche

Cafés and Pubs

1 The Victorian House

MAP C3 ■ Ysenburgstraße 13 ■ Closed Sun eve, Mon & Tue

A British venue offering a fusion of new and traditional English cuisine from breakfast to dinner. Take a seat on the terrace and enjoy the afternoon tea.

2 Volkart

MAP C3 ■ Volkartstraße 15 ■ Closed L, Mon & Sun

Tapas and Mexican cuisine are what it's all about here, including a wide variety of vegetarian options. Outdoor tables are available.

3 Kitchen2Soul

MAP C3 ■ Schlörstraße 1 ■ Closed Sun–Wed ■ www. kitchen2soul.com

This cute café also operates as an independent bookstore. Breakfast here is a highlight, with muesli, avocado toast and fresh pastries on offer. Kitchen2Soul also hosts seminars, creative workshops and training courses.

4 MARITA

MAP C3 ■ Schulstraße 34 ■ (089) 1301 1652

A pretty little café, MARITA offers a long, varied breakfast and lunch menu and locally baked cakes. Outdoor seating is also available.

5 Café Kosmos

MAP L2 ■ Dachauer Straße 7 ■ Closed Sat & Sun L

Situated by the Hauptbahnhof, this bar with a retro charm has a spiral staircase. It is normally very busy so be prepared to wait.

6 Piacere Nuovo

MAP C4 ■ Donnersbergerstraße 54 ■ Closed Mon D, Sat D & Sun

With delicious homemade Italian specialities and wonderfully friendly service, Piacere Nuovo is the right place for both lunch and dinner.

7 Butter

MAP J1 ■ Blutenburgstraße 90 ■ Closed Sat & Sun

A great little bistro serving breakfast, pastries and flavoursome mains.

8 Café Ruffini

MAP C3 ■ Orffstraße 22–4 ■ Closed Mon

A Munich institution, this place was the city's first eco café, serving up tasty organic treats, including wholesome breakfasts and baked goods from its own bakery. Sit on the rooftop terrace, where readings are occasionally held.

Organic Café Ruffini

9 Café Neuhausen

MAP D3 ■ Blutenburgstraße 106

This café, with a stuccoed ceiling and a covered garden, serves breakfast, lunch and dinner (plus Sunday brunch). The menu comprises Italian, Austrian and Bavarian dishes.

10 Sappralott

MAP C3 ■ Donnersbergerstraße 37

An Augustinian guesthouse with dark wood panelling, Sappralott serves Bavarian and international cuisine. Happy hours are from 11pm.

See map on pp126–7

📟 Beyond Munich

Munich is the ideal starting point for excursions to the Upper Bavarian lakes – Ammersee and Starnberger See are the two main lakes in Fünfseenland – or to Chiemsee, known as the "Bavarian Sea". Also within easy reach are a number of ancient monasteries and world-famous churches, including the Wieskirche, a UNESCO World Heritage Site. A visit to at least one of Ludwig's palaces, preferably Neuschwanstein, is essential. It's worth noting that the Alps aren't just for hikers; you can easily reach Germany's highest peak – Zugspitze – in a day, via mountain railway and cable car.

Visitors at the top of the Zugspitze, Germany's highest peak

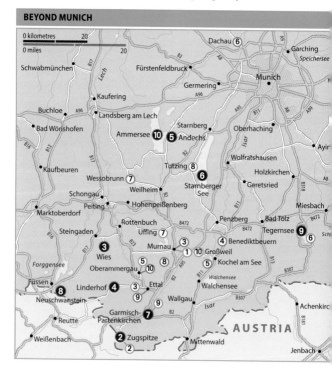

BEYOND MUNICH

Chiemsee with a view of the mountains and islands

1 Chiemsee, Herrenchiemsee and Fraueninsel

Popularly thought of as the "Bavarian Sea", Chiemsee is Bavaria's largest lake, with an area of 80 sq km (31 sq miles). It is home to four islands, the largest of which are Herreninsel and Fraueninsel – the latter has an 8th-century monastery. It is at Herrenchiemsee that you will find the Altes Schloss, an Augustinian monastery, and the Neues Schloss (Schloss Herrenchiemsee), which is said to be Ludwig II's Bavarian equivalent of Versailles. Despite construction beginning in 1878, the Neues Schloss was never completed. Its extravagant staircase and large mirror gallery are particularly impressive. The south wing is home to the King Ludwig II Museum (open daily, see www. herrenchiemsee.de for details).

2 Zugspitze

One of the best ways to enjoy the Zugspitze is to take a round trip on the mountain train and cable car. In Garmisch, the journey begins with the funicular, which takes you to the Schneeferner glacier on the Zugspitzplatt. Here, you switch to a cable car, which ascends to the summit. The observation platform offers a spectacular vista, and on a clear day you can see all the way to the Dolomites. Take the cable car on your way back down to the valley, and you'll be treated to wonderful views of Eibsee, Garmisch-Partenkirchen and Werdenfelser Land.

Rococo interior of the Wieskirche, a UNESCO World Heritage Site

③ Wieskirche
Wies 14, Steingaden ■ (088) 6293 2930 ■ **Open summer: 8am–8pm daily (winter: until 5pm)** ■ **www.wieskirche.de**

Known simply as the Wieskirche, the mid-18th-century Pilgrim Church of the Scourged Saviour is renowned as a prime example of German Rococo. It represents the work of Dominikus Zimmermann at his peak. UNESCO listed the church as a World Heritage Site in 1983.

Ludwig II's Schloss Linderhof

④ Schloss Linderhof
Linderhof 12, Ettal ■ (088) 229 2030 ■ **Open Apr–mid-Oct: 9am–6pm daily; mid-Oct–Mar: 10am–4:30pm daily** ■ **Adm** ■ **www.schlosslinderhof.de**

Schloss Linderhof was originally a hunting lodge belonging to Maximilian II. Ludwig II had it torn down and rebuilt in the park, making it the only palace that was actually completed during his lifetime. The Schlosspark comprises a French garden complete with parterres and terraces, surrounded by a country park. It is home to attractions such as the Marokkanische Haus, Maurische Kiosk, and the famous Venus Grotto (closed for renovation until 2024), where the king liked to be rowed around in a golden boat.

⑤ Kloster Andechs
www.andechs.de

This "holy mountain" stands almost 200 m (656 ft) tall on the east bank of the Ammersee. Founded in 1455 as a Dominican monastery with a Rococo church, it is one of the most significant pilgrimage sites in Bavaria. Its tavern and beer garden attract crowds wanting to try the famous monastery beer, Andechser.

⑥ Starnberger See
Of all the lakes in this area, it was the Starnberger See (21 km/ 13 miles long, 5 km/3 miles wide and up to 127 m/417 ft deep) that became the most popular with the local population. Just like Ammersee, Tegernsee and Königssee, this lake is also home to tour boats from the "Weißblaue Flotte" fleet. Featuring a beautiful rose garden, the Roseninsel is the only island in the middle of the lake and can be easily reached with smaller boats. The lake itself is

surrounded by a number of palaces: "Sisi-Schloss" Possenhofen, Tutzing, Ammerland, and Berg, which was the summer house of the Wittelsbachs. It was near Berg that Ludwig II died under mysterious circumstances just a few metres from the shore, and a memorial cross marks the tragic spot in the lake. The Expressionist collection at the Buchheim Museum (the Museum der Phantasie), north of Bernried, is well worth a visit.

7 Garmisch-Partenkirchen

Located at the base of the Wetterstein massif and the Zugspitze, the capital of Werdenfelser Land is one of the most popular winter sports resorts in the country. In fact, the Winter Olympics were held here in 1936, as were the FIS Alpine World Ski Championships in 1978 and 2011. The buzzing spa town also draws a large number of visitors during the summer months, as its prime location makes it an ideal base for mountain hiking and excursions into the wider region. The town is light on sights, but the main draw here is without doubt the train and cable car ride up Zugspitze.

8 Neuschwanstein

Ludwig II's fairy-tale castle (see pp36–7) is one of the most popular castles in Europe and hence, worth a visit.

9 Tegernsee and Schliersee

Framed by wooded mountains, Tegernsee is one of the largest mountain lakes in Upper Bavaria, with an area of 9 sq km (3.5 sq miles). Its beautiful setting and proximity to Munich have made it a perennially popular holiday destination. Although not as well known, Schliersee is equally attractive. The best way to take in the scenery is with a walk around the lake (7 km/4 miles).

Watersports on the Ammersee

10 Ammersee

The third-largest lake in Bavaria, the Ammersee occupies a glacial basin dating from the Ice Age. On a clear day, the view of the Alps is breathtaking. A variety of activities are available around the banks of the lake, including sailing, rowing, surfing, diving, cycling and walking.

Ludwig II's beautiful Neuschwanstein at sunrise

See map on pp132–3 ←

The Best of the Rest

Wendelstein, a mountain with views as far as the Großglockner in Austria

 Wendelstein
This 1838-m (6030-ft) mountain peak can be reached via the 1912 rack railway, by cable car, or on foot.

② Spitzingsee
This romantic lake is in the Spitzingsee–Tegernsee ski resort.

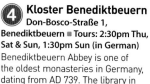 **③ Münter-Haus, Murnau**
Kottmüllerallee 6, Murnau ■ Open 2–5pm Tue–Sun ■ Adm
The Münter-Haus was the summer house of Gabriele Münter and Wassily Kandinsky, and a meeting point for the "Blue Rider" artists.

④ Kloster Benediktbeuern
Don-Bosco-Straße 1, Benediktbeuern ■ Tours: 2:30pm Thu, Sat & Sun, 1:30pm Sun (in German)
Benediktbeuern Abbey is one of the oldest monasteries in Germany, dating from AD 739. The library in the present Baroque complex was once home to the 13th-century *Carmina Burana* manuscript.

⑤ Kochelsee and Walchensee
The Kochelsee and the Walchensee further south are perfect for windsurfing. The Walchensee is the largest and deepest mountain lake in Germany (covering 16 sq km/6 sq miles, and up to 192 m/630 ft deep).

 ⑥ Dachau
Alte Römerstraße 75, Dachau ■ (081) 3166 9970 ■ Open 9am–5pm daily ■ www. kz-gedenkstaette-dachau.de
The first concentration camp was established in 1933 in Dachau (around 20 km/12 miles from Munich). Tours of the memorial site can be booked in advance.

 ⑦ Kloster Wessobrunn
Klosterhof 4, Wessobrunn ■ www.kloster-wessobrunn.de
Wessobrunn stuccowork is renowned internationally. Parts of the monastery are open to the public.

⑧ Murnauer Moos
www.murnau.de
A boardwalk leads into Bavaria's largest continuous moorland, spanning 32 sq km/12 sq miles.

⑨ Kloster Ettal
Kaiser-Ludwig-Platz 1, Ettal
Now a boarding school, this abbey is famous for its herbal liqueur (which can still be bought here).

⑩ Oberammergau
This health resort adorned with Lüftlmalerei frescos is world-famous for its *Passionsspiele*, held every 10 years. The next ones are scheduled for 2032.

Restaurants

PRICE CATEGORIES
Price of a three-course meal (or similar)
for one, with a glass of wine or beer,
including taxes and service.
....
€ below €30   €€ €30–60   €€€ over €60

Alpenhof Murnau
Ramsachstraße 8, Murnau
■ (088) 4149 1320 ■ €€
Upscale Bavarian restaurant with
a panoramic view of the Alps.

Gletscherrestaurant Sonnalpin
www.zugspitze.de ■ €€
This restaurant on the Zugspitzplatt
glacial plateau is, at 2,600 m (8,530 ft),
the highest restaurant in Germany.

3 Klosterhotel Ettal
**Kaiser-Ludwig-Platz 10–12,
Ettal** ■ (088) 229150 ■ €€
Located near Ettal Abbey, a
Benedictine monastery, this res-
taurant serves Bavarian cuisine.

4 Inselhotel zur Linde
Fraueninsel im Chiemsee
■ (080) 549 0366 ■ €€
This traditional, 600-year-old
hotel serves homemade cakes
and Bavarian specialities.

5 Hotel Alte Post
Dorfstraße 19, Oberammergau
■ (088) 229100 ■ €
Set in the town centre, this restaurant
serves Bavarian delicacies.

Outdoor seating at Hotel Alte Post

Herzogliches Bräustüberl Tegernsee

Herzogliches Bräustüberl Tegernsee
Schlossplatz 1, Tegernsee
■ (080) 224141 ■ €
A cosy and rustic Bavarian inn
with a lovely terrace.

7 Seerestaurant Alpenblick
Kirchtalstraße 30, Uffing
■ (088) 469300 ■ **Closed winter:
Thu** ■ €€
The view of the Staffelsee from
the terrace and beer garden is
sensational. Great, seasonal food.

8 Midgardhaus
Midgardstraße 3–5, Tutzing
■ (081) 581216 ■ **Closed Mon** ■ €€
Serving top-notch breakfast
through to dinner on the terrace
overlooking Starnberg See, in the
beer garden, or in the conservatory
of Midgard-Haus.

9 Gasthof zum Rassen
**Ludwigstraße 45, Garmisch-
Partenkirchen** ■ (088) 212089 ■ €
This traditional inn, serving classic
Bavarian fare, is home to Germany's
oldest folk theatre.

10 Kreut-Alm
Kreut 1, Großweil ■ (088)
415822 ■ €
This restaurant offers a breathtaking
panoramic view of the mountains. It
also has a terrace and beer garden.

See map on pp132–3

Streetsmart

Westfriedhof U-Bahn station, with
lighting designed by Ingo Maurer

Getting Around

Arriving by Air

Munich Airport is a major hub for air travel, with most international and domestic airlines passing through. Airlines serving Munich include **Austrian**, **Lufthansa** and **Swiss**. There are shops, restaurants and cafés, and a tourist information centre in the airport. Terminals 1 and 2 house the offices of over 100 airlines.

Located right on the A92, Munich Airport is around 28 km (17 miles) from the city centre. The S-Bahn (S1 & S8) will take you to Marienplatz or the Hauptbahnhof in 40 or 45 minutes, and taxis take the same time provided that the roads are clear.

Most international car rental companies have desks at the airport.

International Train Travel

Regular high-speed international trains connect Germany to various towns and cities in Italy, Austria, France and Eastern Europe. **München Hauptbahnhof** (the city's central station) handles trains to and from Munich. In most cases, there are direct connections to major European cities several times a day. Southern Bavaria is very well connected thanks to its dense rail network.

You can buy tickets and passes for multiple international journeys via **Eurail** or **Interrail**, however, you may still need to pay an additional reservation fee depending on which rail service you travel with. Always check that your pass is valid before boarding.

Regional and Local Trains

Most German trains and railway lines are operated by **Deutsche Bahn AG**. Long-distance routes are served by InterCity Express (ICE), InterCity (IC) and EuroCity (EC) trains, while the network also runs Regional-Express (RE) and RegionalBahn (RB) for shorter distances.

The S-Bahn suburban routes cover a radius of 30–40 km (19–25 miles) around Munich and are ideal for taking day trips to the lakes or to Dachau. The S-Bahn is also an important means of transport within the city centre: its central stretch (11 km/7 miles with all 7 lines) between Donnersbergerbrücke and Ostbahnhof (via Hauptbahnhof, Stachus and Marienplatz) offers connection points to the U-Bahn, buses and trams. During the week, S-Bahn trains run from 4:15am to 1am, every 10 to 20 minutes. On Fridays, Saturdays and some public holidays trains run all night. The majority of S-Bahn stations are wheelchair-accessible.

Public Transport

The **MVG** (Munich Transportation Corporation) and the **MVV** (Munich Traffic and Tariff Association) operate the city's public transport network. Timetables, transport maps, ticket information and mobility services can be obtained from customer service counters in München Hauptbahnhof, **Ostbahnhof** (Munich East train station) and Marienplatz. The MVG and MVV websites also feature a wealth of information, as well as interactive journey planners.

Tickets

All public transport operated by the MVG and the MVV (S-bahn and U-Bahn trains as well as trams and buses) uses the same tickets. These can be bought at ticket machines in U-Bahn and S-Bahn stations, on trams and buses or online as a mobile ticket. Several ticket types are available: multi-ride (streifenkarten), single-ride (einzelkarten), daily passes (tageskarten), weekly passes (wochenkarten) and monthly passes (monatskarten). Multi-ride tickets have to be validated for each zone (zone 1 is Munich's central zone). A normal journey uses 2 strips, while a short journey uses just 1 strip.

Visitors may wish to take advantage of special rates, for example with the **CityTourCard**, which is available for individuals or groups (up to 5 people; children count as a half person), is valid for all forms of public transport and includes reduced entry to over 60 attractions. These tickets can be purchased from ticket machines, tourist information centres or online.

U-Bahn

The U-Bahn underground rail network runs modern trains around the city. Nearly all of its stations are wheelchair-accessible. Seven lines are currently in operation within the city zone (the U8 is only intended as a booster line). In total, the network spans over 100 km (62 miles) and comprises over 100 stations. Like the S-Bahn train network, U-Bahn trains run from 4:15am to 1am daily and arrive every 5 to 10 minutes. On Fridays and Saturdays, and during some public holidays, U-Bahn trains run all through the night.

Trams

Munich's tram network dates from 1876, when horsecars were used to transport locals around the city. Today, the network comprises 13 daytime and 4 nighttime electric tram lines. The daytime lines operate from 4:45am to 1:30am while the nighttime lines operate from 1:30am to 4:30am daily. The network runs in part on accelerated routes. Some lines are perfect for sightseeing (19 goes through the Old Town, for example, and the 25 runs to Grünwald taking a particularly scenic route). Most tram cars have ramps to allow wheelchair access.

Buses

Munich has an extensive bus network that covers most corners of the city and connects travellers to S-Bahn and U-Bahn services. Most buses operate from 5am, to 1am, departing every 10 to 20 minutes. Night buses, recognizable from the "N" in front of the line number, operate throughout the night. The 100 bus (Museumslinie) runs past Munich's most popular museums and is a common route for visitors. Buses are usually equipped with air conditioning as well as low floors and ramps for wheelchair users.

Long-Distance Bus Travel

Many long-distance buses arrive at and depart from the central bus terminal – **Zentraler Omnibusbahnhof (ZOB)** – at the Hackerbrücke. Tourist hotspots in Upper Bavaria (and even some out-of-the-way destinations) are well served by a network of regional bus routes managed by the **Regionalverkehr Oberbayern**. **Flixbus** offers low-cost intercity travel in Europe.

Taxis

You can book a taxi by telephone, hail one or join a queue at a taxi rank. Official taxis in Munich are cream-coloured and have a TAXI sign on the roof. The minimum charge is €4.70, then €2 per km €1.70/€1.60 after 5/10 km). A taxi to the city centre from the airport costs around €50. Taxi services in the city include **Taxi München eG**, **Isar-Funk** and **Taxi Zentrale Freising**. Uber also operates in Munich.

Driving to Munich

Driving licences issued by any of the European Union member states are valid throughout the EU. If visiting from outside the EU, you may need to apply for an International Driving Permit. Always check with your local automobile association before you travel.

Motorways and regional roads are well maintained and easy to navigate in Germany. Six motorways lead into Munich: the A8 Stuttgart/Salzburg, A95 Garmisch-Partenkirchen, A9 Nuremberg/Berlin, A92 Deggendorf, A96 Lindau, and A94 Passau. The Autobahnring ring road (A99, incomplete) lets you bypass the city in part. If you plan to drive into the city, you will need to take two additional ring roads: the Mittlerer Ring and, once you reach the centre, the Altstadtring.

In case of breakdown, contact the **ADAC** (German motoring club) for roadside assistance; club members get discounted rates.

Car Rental

Car-hire firms can be found at Munich airport and at the city's main railway stations. Popular companies such as **Hertz**, **Avis**, **Sixt** and **Budget** all have bases in Munich. In order to rent a vehicle, drivers need to produce their passport, driving licence and a credit card with enough capacity to cover the excess.

Most rental agencies require drivers to be over the age of 21 and to have an international licence.

Driving in Munich

In 2008, Munich, like many other cities in Germany, introduced an **Environmental Green Zone** *(Umweltzonen)*. This only allows vehicles with an *Umweltplakette* (environmental badge) access to the zone, which encompasses the city centre. You will need to obtain this permit prior to travelling here by car. It can be bought online or from any participating garage in Germany.

Parking

One of the biggest challenges for drivers in Munich is finding a parking space. Although there are many multi-storey car parks *(parkhäus)*, they are expensive and often full. ("*frei*" indicates that spaces are available.) Most hotels have some form of parking on offer, but this can come at an additional cost. The majority of on-street parking must be paid for, either by inserting coins into a meter or by buying a pay-and-display ticket. Another issue is the time limit: 1 hour is often the maximum in the centre. Parking attendants issue fines when cars are illegally parked or parking is unpaid. Illegally parked cars can be towed; retrieving them can be expensive and difficult.

Rules of the Road

Drive on the right. Unless otherwise signposted, vehicles coming from the right have priority.

At all times, drivers must carry a valid driver's licence, registration and insurance documents. The wearing of seat belts is compulsory for drivers and passengers. Lights must be used in tunnels and the use of a mobile phone while driving is prohibited – with the exception of a hands-free system.

All drivers must have third-party insurance *(haftpflflichtversicherung)* – it is the minimum insurance requirement in Germany. Drivers will be fined for speeding, tailgating and for committing parking offences. The drink-drive limit *(p145)* is strictly enforced. If you are drinking alcohol, use public transport or take a taxi.

Cycling

Munich is a bicycle-friendly city with plenty of cycle paths. The city centre is largely flat and easy to navigate, with cycle lanes marked on pavements and on the edges of roads. Bicycle stands are situated throughout the city, including large facilities at railway and S-Bahn stations. Bicycles should always be locked to an immovable object.

Bicycles can be taken on the U-Bahn and S-Bahn in the last carriage marked with a cycle logo, except at rush hour from 6am to 9am and 4pm to 6pm. In addition to a regular passenger ticket, you will need to buy a one-day Farrad-Tageskarte for €2.60. You cannot take your bike on the city's trams or buses, unless it is a fold-up bike.

The various bike-rental options available include the **MVG Rad** system, which provides 1,200 bicycles across 125 stations, the **Call a Bike** system and **Pedalhelden**.

Like drivers, cyclists must travel on the right. If in doubt, dismount: many novices cross busy junctions on foot; if you do so, switch to the pedestrian section of the crossing. Beware of tram tracks; cross them at an angle to avoid getting stuck. For your own safety do not walk with your bike in a bike lane or cycle on pavements, on the side of the road or in the dark without lights. Wearing a helmet is recommended when cycling in the city, but it is not a legal requirement in Germany. Drink-drive limits here also apply to cyclists.

Tourist offices provide cycle maps of Munich with routes of the best cycling tours. Avid cyclists can also venture further into Bavaria for tougher routes through the Bavarian Alps.

Walking

The best way to explore Munich is on foot. Much of the Old Town has been closed to traffic and many of the main tourist attractions are within a 20-minute walk of one another.

Visitors can escape the urban bustle with a walk through one of Munich's many parks. In summer, paths along the Isar River lead you through lush greenery to beaches filled with sun-bathers.

The Bavarian Alps promise some particularly lovely walks. Numerous paths are well marked along rivers, through forests and up mountains. The foothills of the Alps provide some easy terrain for gentle hikes but the higher you go the more demanding it becomes. Note that bad weather can strike at any time, so planning and good preparation are essential. Ensure you have suitable hiking boots, warm waterproof clothing, a map and a compass. Tell someone where you're going and when you plan to return.

Guided Tours

Munich has a wide variety of guided walking and cycle tours, usually with hired bikes provided. You may be able to just show up and join a scheduled tour, but it is advisable to reserve ahead. Some of the best trips are given by **Radius Tours**, located within a bike-rental shop in the Hauptbahnhof. Daily themed tours (in English) last around 2 hours and cover the major historical sights.

Tours in open-topped buses run by **Münchner Stadtrundfahrten** require less energy.

Practical Information

Passports and Visas

For entry requirements, including visas, consult your nearest German embassy or check the **German Federal Foreign Office** website. EU nationals and citizens of the UK, US, Canada, Australia and New Zealand do not need visas for stays of up to three months. Germany has reinstated ad hoc passport checks at some of its land borders, so always make sure you have your ID with you.

Government Advice

Now more than ever, it is important to consult both your and the German government's advice before travelling. The **UK Foreign, Commonwealth and Development Office (FCDO)**, the **US State Department**, the **Australian Department of Foreign Affairs and Trade** and the German Federal Foreign Office offer the latest information on security, health and local regulations.

Customs Information

You can find information on the laws relating to goods and currency taken in or out of Germany on the Federal Customs Service (**Zoll**) website.

Insurance

We strongly recommend taking out a comprehensive insurance policy covering theft, loss of belongings, medical care, cancellations and delays, and make sure you read the small print very carefully.

UK citizens are eligible for free emergency medical care in Germany provided they have a valid European Health Insurance Card (EHIC) or UK Global Health Insurance Card (**GHIC**).

Vaccinations

There are no legal immunization requirements for visiting Germany. For information regarding COVID-19 vaccination requirements, consult government advice.

Health

Germany has a world-class health service. EU citizens are eligible to receive emergency medical treatment in Germany free of charge. If you have an EHIC or GHIC present this as soon as possible.

For visitors from outside the EU, payment of medical expenses is the patient's responsibility. It is important to arrange comprehensive medical insurance before travel.

Munich has excellent hospitals. Some of the clinics attached to the university, including the **Chirurgische Klinik und Poliklinik**, occupy a central location and have emergency departments. Some clinics, such as the **Klinikum Schwabing**, have dedicated paediatric emergency departments.

Chemists are easy to spot with their red "A" (for *apotheke*) signs, and usually stay open until 7 or 8pm. Following this time, every chemist displays the details of other chemists in the area offering an emergency evening or weekend service. An **emergency service portal** online also shows details of the nearest chemist.

Smoking, Alcohol and Drugs

Germany has a smoking ban in all public places, including bars, cafés, restaurants and hotels. However, some establishments circumvent these laws by calling themselves a *raucherkneipe*, or smoking pub.

The possession of narcotics is prohibited and could result in prosecution and prison.

Unless stated otherwise, it is permitted to drink alcohol on the streets and in public parks and gardens. Germany has a strict limit of 0.05 per cent BAC (blood alcohol content) for drivers.

ID

There is no requirement for visitors to carry ID, but in the event of a routine check you may be asked to show your passport. If you don't have it with you, the police may escort you to wherever your passport is being kept.

Personal Security

Munich has one of the lowest crime rates in the whole of Europe.

However, pickpockets still operate in busy tourist areas and on public transport. Keep valuables out of sight and take extra care during Oktoberfest.

If you have anything stolen, report the crime as soon as possible to the nearest police station. Get a copy of the crime report in order to claim on your insurance. Contact your embassy if you have your passport stolen, or in the event of a serious crime or accident.

The **police** and **medical services** in Germany have dedicated numbers, but you can also call the **European Emergency Number** which covers the fire and ambulance services. Munich also has a **women's emergency hotline** and an **emergency dentist** number.

Germans are generally accepting of all people, regardless of their race, gender or sexuality. The country officially legalized homosexuality in 1994 and same-sex marriage has been legal since 2017. Despite the freedoms that the LGBTQ+ community enjoy, acceptance is not always a given. If you do feel unsafe at any time, the **Safe Space Alliance** pinpoints your nearest place of refuge. **Diversity** also runs a youth centre and café offering support to the LGBTQ+ community.

Travellers with Specific Requirements

Germany is ahead of the curve when it comes to barrier-free travel. Most S-Bahn and U-Bahn stations, trams and buses are accessible for those with specific requirements. Special city tours also operate for those who are hearing impaired (available in international sign language) and visually impaired.

The **Club Behinderter und ihrer Freunde** (Club for the Disabled and Friends or CBF) provides information on accessible cinemas, theatres and museums. It also organizes events and offers support for cultural events. Additional advice and information about wheelchair rentals is also available online from **VDK Bayern**. The city's tourism website, **Simply Munich**, provides a list of venues which have special access.

Visitors should be aware that several areas in the city have original cobblestone paving, which may prove difficult to traverse for wheelchair users. Similarly, some restaurants in old buildings may have limited access.

DIRECTORY

PASSPORTS AND VISAS

German Federal Foreign Office
🌐 auswaertiges-amt.de

GOVERNMENT ADVICE

Australian Department of Foreign Affairs and Trade
🌐 dfat.gov.au
🌐 smartraveller.gov.au

UK Foreign, Commonwealth and Development Office (FCDO)
🌐 gov.uk/foreign-travel-advice

US State Department
🌐 travel.state.gov

CUSTOMS INFORMATION

Zoll
🌐 zoll.de

INSURANCE

GHIC
🌐 ghic.org.uk

HEALTH

Chirurgische Klinik und Poliklinik
MAP L4
■ Nußbaumstraße 20
📞 (089) 4400-52647

Emergency Service Portal
🌐 lak-bayern notdienst-portal.de

Klinikum Schwabing
MAP F1 ■ Kölner Platz 1
📞 (089) 30680
For children: Parzivalstraße 16 📞 (089) 30 682589

PERSONAL SECURITY

Diversity
🌐 diversity-muenchen.de

Emergency Dentist
📞 (089) 5790 9596

European Emergency Number
📞 112

Medical Services
📞 116 117

Police
📞 110

Safe Space Alliance
🌐 safespacealliance.com

Women's Emergency Hotline
📞 (089) 763737

TRAVELLERS WITH SPECIFIC REQUIREMENTS

Club Behinderter und ihrer Freunde
📞 (089) 3 568808

Simply Munich
🌐 muenchen-tourismus-barrierefrei.de

VDK Bayern
🌐 vdk.de

Time Zone

Munich uses Central European Time (CET), and Germany observes daylight-savings summer time from the end of March to the end of October, like its neighbouring countries.

Money

Germany is one of the 19 European countries using the euro (€). Most establishments accept major credit, debit and prepaid currency cards. Contactless payments have become the norm since the COVID-19 pandemic, though they are not generally used on public transport. It is always worth carrying cash, as some smaller restaurants and beer gardens don't accept card.

A tip of 5–10 per cent is customary if service is particularly good.

Electrical Appliances

Power sockets are type C and F, both fitting two-pronged plugs. Standard voltage is 230 volts.

Mobile Phones and Wi-Fi

Deutsche Telekom is the provider for public telephones. Visitors travelling to Germany with EU tariffs can use their mobile phones abroad without being affected by data roaming charges; instead they will be charged the same rates for data, SMS and voice calls as they would pay at home. Visitors from other countries should check their contracts before using their phone in Germany in order to avoid unexpected charges.

Network providers T-Mobile, Vodafone and O2 cover Munich and Bavaria, and coverage is generally good except in remote areas, such as in the Alps. Mobile phones can be used on the S-Bahn and even on the U-Bahn without any issues.

High-speed internet and Wi-Fi is available in cafés and hotels across the city. Tourist areas such as the Deutsches Museum, Marienplatz, Karlsplatz/Stachus, Münchner Freiheit and Odeonsplatz also have free Wi-Fi hotspots. A list of the city's free **Wi-Fi hotspots** can be found on Munich's official website. Note that the German for Wi-Fi is W-Lan (pronounced *veh-lan*).

Postal Services

German post offices and post boxes are easy to spot with their distinctive yellow Deutsche Post signs. Munich's post offices are very much in decline though, as retailers (partner branches) such as **Postbank Finanzcenter** have started to take over the service. As a result, many of the architecturally interesting post office buildings have become shopping centres.

Stamps *(briefmarke)* can be bought in post offices, newsagents, tobacconists and most major supermarkets. Postcards cost €0.45 to send within Germany, and €0.90 internationally. Postage for letters is €0.70/€0.90.

Weather

Visitors can expect mild and sometimes rainy days in spring. Summer brings clear blue skies and locals flock outside to enjoy the sun. The heaviest rainfall, however, occurs in the summer so visitors should come prepared for sudden downpours. It is not unknown for the region to experience unseasonably warm weather during autumn, and this is its best time for hiking tours around the area. Autumn also often sees the notorious Föhn, a warm, dry, downslope wind, sweeping in from the Alps. Winters here are unpredictable. They may be icy and snowy or mild and snowfree.

Opening Hours

Most shops in the centre are open Monday to Saturday, 9am to 8pm, though the subject of relaxing or abolishing the law regulating opening hours is still a matter of debate in the city. Offices, banks and post offices tend to close earlier, usually by 4, 5 or 6pm.

The COVID-19 pandemic proved that situations can change suddenly. Always check before visiting attractions and hospitality venues for up-to-date hours and booking requirements.

Visitor Information

Munich's **tourist board** has two visitor information centres: one on **Marienplatz** and the other at **München Hauptbahnhof**. Here, visitors can access all sorts of information and services, from city maps and brochures to tickets or room reservations. There's also another information centre at Alten Hof, in the Old Town, as well as the main desk at Munich Airport.

If you are interested in visiting the surrounding countryside, local tourist offices in the various districts are useful resources.

Tickets for the theatre or music concerts can generally bought from the relevant ticket offices. Telephone numbers for these can be found throughout this guide.

Alternatively, **München Ticket** and **ZKV München** offer advance tickets for most events. Advance ticket points also exist at the Rathaus (town hall) and the information pavilion at the Olympia Eishalle arena. You will also find advance booking centres on the lower floor of the S-Bahn station at Marienplatz and on the lower floor of Stachus.

Local Customs

Germany has strict laws on hate speech and symbols linked to the Nazis. Disrespectful behaviour in public places can warrant a fine, or even prosecution. Pay close attention to signage indicating when photos aren't allowed and think carefully about how you compose your shots. Visitors have come under serious criticism for posting inappropriate photos taken at sites of national significance on social media.

Language

German is the official language in Munich, but English is widely spoken throughout the city. You can generally get by knowing little German, but a few niceties in the local language are usually appreciated. English is less commonly spoken outside the city center and in the Bavarian Alps. When travelling here you may still encounter people who speak only German, so it is advisable to learn some practical phrases before you visit.

Taxes and Refunds

VAT is 19 per cent in Germany. Non-EU residents are entitled to a tax refund subject to certain conditions. In order to obtain this, you must request a tax receipt and export papers (*Ausfuhrbescheinigung*) when you purchase your goods. When leaving the country, present these papers, along with the receipt and your ID, at customs to receive your refund.

Accommodation

Hotel prices in Munich are generally higher than in the rest of Bavaria, although breakfast is often included. There are plenty of affordable places too, including small hotels, serviced apartments and B&Bs. Prices vary according to the season and are particularly expensive during Oktoberfest, although many hotels do have reduced weekend rates and lower prices during the off-season.

The Bavarian Alps also offer a variety of accomodation options, ranging from rooms in romantic castles to local guesthouses and campsites.

Bookings can be made over the phone or online. Be aware that hotel bookings around Oktoberfest time should be made a year in advance. Staying outside of Munich and commuting in can save you a small amount.

DIRECTORY

MOBILE PHONES AND WI-FI

Wi-Fi Hotspots
W muenchen.de

POSTAL SERVICES

Postbank Finanzcenter
MAP L3 ■ Bahnhofsplatz 1 ■ Open 8am–7pm Mon–Fri, 9am–3pm Sat

VISITOR INFORMATION

München Hauptbahnhof
MAP L3 ■ Bahnhofsplatz 2

Marienplatz
MAP N3 ■ Neues Rathaus, Marienplatz 8
C (089) 2339 6500

München Ticket
MAP N3 ■ Rathaus (Dienerstraße entrance)
W muenchenticket.de

Tourist Board
MAP M4 ■ Sendlinger Straße 1 W muenchen.de

ZKV München
MAP N3 ■ Marienplatz, lower floor W zkv-muenchen.de

Places to Stay

PRICE CATEGORIES

For a standard double room per night (with breakfast if included), taxes and service.

€ under €100 €€ €100–200 €€€ over €200

Luxury Hotels

Bayerischer Hof

MAP M3 ▪ Promenade-platz 2–6 ▪ (089) 21200 ▪ www.bayerischerhof.de ▪ €€€

Now in the hands of the fourth generation, this privately-owned luxury hotel, dating back to 1841, offers 340 rooms and suites, 40 banquet rooms, five restaurants (the three-Michelin-starred Atelier, plus Garden, Palais Keller and Trader Vic's) and six bars. Limited access for those with specific requirements.

The Charles Hotel

MAP L2 ▪ Sophienstraße 28 ▪ (089) 544 5550 ▪ www.roccofortehotels.com ▪ €€€

A member of the Rocco Forte group, this luxury five-star hotel can be found next to the Alter Botanischer Garten, not far from Karlsplatz. Built on the site of an old university library, rooms are modern and spacious. It also offers a restaurant with terrace, spa, gym and conference rooms.

Hotel Vier Jahreszeiten Kempinski

MAP N3 ▪ Maximilianstr. 17 ▪ (089) 21250 ▪ www.kempinski.com ▪ €€€

The 316 air-conditioned rooms and suites in this hotel ooze elegance and luxury. The Schwarzreiter restaurant – named after Ludwig II's favourite fish dish of deepwater char – offers modern Bavarian cuisine. Wellness area available.

Mandarin Oriental

MAP N3 ▪ Neuturm-straße 1 ▪ (089) 290980 ▪ www.mandarinoriental.com ▪ €€€

First-class service and historic ambience near Maximilianstraße. This five-star hotel has 53 rooms and 20 suites, as well as banqueting and conference facilities. The rooftop terrace with pool affords fabulous views over the old town. The latest in its impressive line-up of restaurants and bars is Matsuhisa (see p65) – the only restaurant in Germany to be headed up by celebrated Japanese chef, Nobu Matsuhisa.

Sofitel Munich Bayerpost

MAP K3 ▪ Bayerstraße 12 ▪ (089) 599480 ▪ www.sofitel.com ▪ €€€

This five-star hotel has been created behind the historic façade of a Wilhelmine post office building and offers a contemporary and elegant setting for banquets or conferences. The extensive spa area, well-equipped gym and an exclusive restaurant all combine to make a stay at this hotel a truly luxurious experience.

Business Hotels

Hilton Munich City

MAP Q5 ▪ Rosenheimer Straße 15 ▪ (089) 48040 ▪ www.hilton.com ▪ €€

Offering well-appointed rooms and suites, this hotel is situated by the Gasteig cultural centre. Guests can take advantage of seven meeting rooms with variable seating options, as well as a large ballroom, ideal for hosting events. It also has two restaurants, a bar and café, and a gym. The hotel has limited access for those with specific requirements.

IntercityHotel München

MAP L3 ▪ Bayerstraße 10 ▪ (0) 444440 ▪ www.intercityhotel.de ▪ €€

Right by the Hauptbahnhof, this hotel offers comfortable, sound-proofed rooms. Free Wi-Fi is available in the seven meeting rooms and in the guest rooms. There's also a restaurant and bar. Limited access for those with specific requirements.

Mövenpick Hotel München-Airport

Ludwigstraße 43, Hallbergmoos ▪ (0) 811 8880 ▪ www.movenpick.com ▪ €€

This state-of-the-art, four-star conference hotel is just minutes away from Munich Airport. It offers comfortable, soundproofed rooms with Wi-Fi, plus ten conference rooms. There is also a restaurant and a beer garden where guests can unwind. The hotel has limited access for people with specific requirements.

Hilton Munich Airport Hotel

Terminalstraße Mitte 20, Oberding ▪ (089) 97820 ▪ www.hilton.com ▪ €€€

The main attraction of this hotel is its atrium, lined with 20-m (65-ft) high palm trees and with a view of the runway – an ideal backdrop for receptions, exhibitions and presentations. The bedrooms are spacious and furnished to the highest standard. It also has a business centre, spa and wellness area, and a gym. Breakfast is not included. Access within the hotel is limited for those with specific requirements.

Marriott Hotel München

MAP G1 ▪ Berliner Straße 93 ▪ (089) 360020 ▪ www.marriott.de ▪ €€€

This hotel with 348 rooms and suites, has a business and tech-enabled conference rooms, making it ideal for business travellers. There is also a pool and a spa, perfect to relax in at the end of a long day. The hotel has limited access for guests with specific requirements.

Mid-Range Hotels

Alpen Hotel München

MAP L3 ▪ Adolf-Kolping-Straße 14 ▪ (089) 559330 ▪ www.alpenhotel-muenchen.de ▪ €€

Located on a side street, this hotel is close to the pedestrian zone without being noisy. The 55 four-star rooms and junior suites all have Wi-Fi. The menu at its in-house restaurant, Stefan, offers a combination of Mediterranean and Bavarian cooking. There is also

a beautiful courtyard garden to relax in. Limited access for those with specific requirements.

Eurostars Grand Central

MAP J2 ▪ Arnulfstraße 35 ▪ (089) 516 5740 ▪ www.eurostarshotels.de ▪ €€

Offering all the latest technical innovations, this hotel has 229 double rooms, 15 triples, eight suites and ten apartments for longer stays. There's also a pool, sauna, terrace and tapas restaurant.

Hotel Admiral

MAP N5 ▪ Kohlstraße 9 ▪ (089) 216350 ▪ www.hotel-admiral.de ▪ €€

This four-star hotel opposite the Deutsches Museum has 32 cosy, individually styled rooms and beautiful gardens that create a relaxing atmosphere. Pets are welcome, and some smoking rooms are available. There is an organic breakfast buffet.

Hotel Europäischer Hof

MAP L3 ▪ Bayerstraße 31 ▪ (089) 551510 ▪ www.heh.de ▪ €€

This three-star hotel is located opposite the Hauptbahnhof. There's a breakfast buffet, handy underground parking and special deals for children. Pets are welcome. All rooms have Internet access, and there's also a meeting room available.

Hotel Gio

MAP L5 ▪ Häberlstraße 9 ▪ (089) 5999 3901 ▪ www.hotel-herzog-muenchen.com ▪ €€

Eighty comfortable and stylish rooms await guests at this hotel, which is

conveniently located next to the Goetheplatz U-Bahn station. Most rooms have their own balcony with a view over the idyllic inner courtyard garden. Breakfast is not included.

Hotel Ibis München City Arnulfpark

MAP J2 ▪ Arnulfstraße 55 ▪ (089) 232 4930 ▪ www.ibis.com ▪ €€

A member of the Accor Group, this hotel offers 204 air-conditioned rooms (including ten rooms for guests with special access requirements). It is located a stone's throw from the Hauptbahnhof and offers easy access to the city centre – the tram stop is right outside.

Hotel Leopold

MAP G2 ▪ Leopoldstr. 119 ▪ (089) 367061 ▪ www.hotel-leopold.de ▪ €€

The classic style and idyllic garden at this traditional hotel in the heart of Schwabing, reflect the efforts of a family-run operation. All 100 rooms offer four-star comfort. Special beds for allergy sufferers are available on request. The hotel has limited access for those with specific requirements.

Hotel Seibel

MAP J4 ▪ Theresienhöhe 9 ▪ (089) 540 1420 ▪ www.seibel-hotels-munich.de ▪ €€

This three-star, Art Nouveau hotel, offers 50 comfortable rooms (including triples and quads) with free Wi-Fi. Some rooms have a balcony overlooking Theresienwiese. There are special rates for same-day bookings.

Leonardo Hotel

MAP L3 ▪ Senefelder-
straße 4 ▪ (089) 551540
▪ www.leonardo-hotels.
com ▪ €€
Situated close to the
Hauptbahnhof, this
hotel offers 80 modern
rooms with free Wi-Fi.
Serves an organic break-
fast. There is parking,
although it is subject
to a charge.

Arthotel Munich

MAP K3 ▪ Paul-Heyse-
Straße 10 ▪ (089) 592122
▪ www.arthotelmunich.
com ▪ €€€
Occupying a beautiful,
centrally-located Art
Nouveau building, the
Arthotel is stylishly
appointed throughout.
It is convenient for all
forms of public transport.
Parking is available
within the building.

Hotels with Flair

Moma 1890

MAP R5 ▪ Orleansplatz
6A ▪ (089) 448 2424
▪ www.moma1890.com
▪ €€
Every room in this hotel
dating back to 1890 is
unique. The beds have
orthopaedic mattresses
for a great night's sleep.
Offers a superb breakfast
with free-range eggs.

Holiday Inn

MAP H6 ▪ Leuchtenber-
gring 20 ▪ (089) 189
0860 ▪ www.ihg.com
▪ €€
The hallmark of this
hotel is its leafy courtyard
where guests can relax
after a long day. The
rooms here are sound-
proofed and all eight
meeting rooms are air
conditioned. There is also
a bar on site. Access is
limited for those with
specific requirements.

Hotel Marienbad

MAP M2 ▪ Barer Straße
11 ▪ (089) 595585 ▪ www.
hotelmarienbad.de ▪ €€
Once the haunt of
illustrious personalities
such as Puccini and
Wagner, the grand old
Marienbad has been
around for centuries.
Today, it is a mid-range,
characterful hotel with
a good restaurant and
modern bathrooms.

Cortiina Hotel

MAP N4 ▪ Ledererstraße
8 ▪ (089) 242 2490
▪ www.cortiina.com
▪ €€€
A stylish city hotel with
an individual style. The
interiors of the 33 rooms
are finished with natural
wood and stone, linen
and leather. The bar is a
fashionable destination
for cocktails.

Flushing Meadows

MAP M5 ▪ Fraunhofer-
straße 32 ▪ (089) 5527
9170 ▪ www.flushing
meadowshotel.com ▪ €€€
Located on the top two
floors of an industrial
building, this trendy hotel
in the city's Glockenbach
quarter offers loft studios
and penthouses complete
with terraces. It is also
home to a popular roof-
top bar. Bikes for hire are
available at no extra cost.

H'Otello

MAP N4 ▪ Baaderstraße 1
▪ (089) 4583 1200 ▪ www.
hotello.de/b01-muenchen
▪ €€€
The perfect choice
for design purists, the
H'Otello is a sophisticated
hotel located near the
Isartor. Its impressive
rooftop terrace provides
an incredible view of the
city centre, and its central
location makes it ideal for
shopping and sightseeing.

Budget Hotels

Hotel Markt

MAP N4 ▪ Heiliggeist-
straße 6 ▪ (089) 225
014 ▪ www.hotel-am-
markt.eu ▪ €
This half-timbered hotel
is located just around the
corner from the lively
Marienplatz. The rooms
are clean and simple and
staff are friendly. Be sure
to visit the restaurant, too.

Hotel Garni Lex im Gartenhof

MAP L2 ▪ Briennertraße
48 ▪ (089) 542 7260
▪ www.hotel-lex.de ▪ €
Situated in a secluded
courtyard, this friendly
hotel with simple yet
modern rooms is the
only hotel in the museum
quarter within walking
distance of all the muse-
ums. Apartments are also
available for those who
wish to stay for longer.

Hotel Royal

MAP L3 ▪ Schillerstraße
11a ▪ (089) 5998 8160
▪ www.hotel-royal.de ▪ €
This centrally located
three-star hotel has 40
non-smoking rooms with
soundproofed windows.
Family and shared rooms
are available and there
is free Wi-Fi.

Motel One München-Sendlinger Tor

MAP M4 ▪ Herzog-
Wilhelm-Straße 28 ▪ (089)
51 77 72 50 ▪ www.motel-
one.com ▪ €
This budget hotel with
a designer twist is a real

gem. The "Sendlinger Tor" building is set right in the heart of the old town, and plenty of attractions are located within walking distance. There is free Wi-Fi but breakfast is not included in the room rate. There is limited access for those with specific requirements.

Hotel Blauer Bock

MAP M3 ▪ Sebastiansplatz 9 ▪ (089) 231780 ▪ www.hotelblauerbock. de ▪ €€
This family-run hotel is right next to Viktualienmarkt. The 400-year-old house is brimming with old-world Munich charm and also incorporates a traditional restaurant of the same name. Parking is available.

Hostels, B&Bs and Apartments

Bed & Breakfast München

www.bedandbreakfast. de/muenchen ▪ €
This company offers an alternative to hotel rooms, namely guest rooms and apartments with or without breakfast for stays from one night to weeks or even months.

Concept Living Munich

Pfälzer-Wald-Straße 2 ▪ (089) 6600 8910 ▪ www.concept-living-munich.de ▪ €
Seven apartment-style spaces, located in the Giesing quarter, are available for one to eight people. The rooms offered here have modern decor and furnishings with a kitchen and bathroom.

Other facilities include DVD players in rooms and Internet access.

Euro Youth Hotel Munich

MAP L3 ▪ Senefelderstraße 5 ▪ (089) 599 0880 ▪ www.euro-youth-hotel.de ▪ €
The bedrooms and dorms at this centrally located hostel are wonderfully bright and roomy. Wi-Fi is available, and breakfast is included with single and double rooms. There is a Euro bar with live music at weekends, and happy hours are from 5:30 to 9pm.

Jaeger's Hostel

MAP L3 ▪ Senefelderstraße 3 ▪ (089) 555 281 ▪ www.jaegers hotel.de ▪ €
This colourful hostel, located a stone's throw from Munich Central Station, offers the full range of room types from dorms through to singles with en-suite bathrooms. There is free Wi-Fi and a bar on site.

Meininger Munich City Centre

MAP D4 ▪ Landsberger Straße 20 ▪ (089) 5499 8023 ▪ www.meininger-hotels.com ▪ €
Set near the main train station, this basic hotel plus hostel offers dorms as well as single and double rooms. Its location and transport connections make it a great option.

Smart Stay Hostel Munich City

MAP L4 ▪ Mozartstraße 4 ▪ (089) 558 7970 ▪ www.smart-stay.de ▪ €
Near Goetheplatz, this hostel (which has a sister

building at Schützenstraße 7) offers single and double rooms with bathrooms, as well as dorms. Additional features include a small self-service kitchen, bar, restaurant and bicycle hire. There is limited access for those with specific requirements.

Wombat's City Hostel Munich

MAP L3 ▪ Senefelderstraße 1 ▪ (089) 5998 9180 ▪ www.wombats-hostels.com ▪ €
This hostel near the Hauptbahnhof offers a combination of dorms and double bedrooms – all with showers and lockers. There is also a glass-roofed courtyard brimming with plants. Wi-Fi is free. There is limited access for those with specific requirements.

Augustin

Am Bavariapark 16 ▪ (089) 5108 8310 ▪ www. augustin-hotel.com ▪ €
A reasonably priced, family-friendly hotel, Augustin has a welcoming atmosphere and reasonable prices. It is located near the Theresienwiese, venue for Oktoberfest.

Maximilian Munich Apartments & Hotel

MAP N4 ▪ Hochbrückenstraße 18 ▪ (089) 242580 ▪ www.maximilian-munich.com ▪ €€€
The accommodation options here include 54 studios, suites and apartments in the main building and two summer houses in the rose garden. All of the options come complete with a sleeping and living area. There's also a restaurant and bar.

For a key to hotel price categories see p148

General Index

Acknowledgments

This edition updated by

Contributor Marc Di Duca
Senior Editor Alison McGill
Senior Designer Stuti Tiwari
Project Editors Parnika Bagla, Lucy Sara-Kelly
Assistant Editor Riddhi Garg
Picture Research Administrator Vagisha Pushp
Picture Research Manager Taiyaba Khatoon
Publishing Assistant Halima Mohammed
Jacket Designer Jordan Lambley
Senior Cartographer Mohammad Hassan
Cartography Manager Suresh Kumar
Senior DTP Designer Tanveer Zaidi
Senior Production Editor Jason Little
Production Controller Manjit Sihra
Deputy Managing Editor Beverly Smart
Managing Editors Shikha Kulkarni,
Hollie Teague
Managing Art Editor Sarah Snelling
Senior Managing Art Editor Priyanka Thakur
Art Director Maxine Pedliham
Publishing Director Georgina Dee

DK would like to thank the following for
their contribution to the previous editions:
Andiamo! Language Services, Hilary Bird,
Dr Elfi Ledig, Clare Peel

The publisher would like to thank the
following for their kind permission to
reproduce their photographs:
Key: a-above; b-below/bottom;
c-centre; f-far; l-left; r-right; t-top
Alamy Stock Photo: age fotostock / Howard
Stapleton 108cla; ALLTRAVEL / Peter Mross
4cla; Arcaid Images / Nigel Young / Foster &
Partners 97tl; Art Kowalsky 24–5; Bildarchiv
Monheim GmbH / Florian Monheim 106tl;
Timo Christ 34–5c; DanitaDelimont.com /
Martin Zwick 90tl; dpa picture alliance Archive /
Frank Leonhardt 60b; filmfoto-03edit 75cl;
Peter Forsberg 22crb; Dennis Hallinan 96cla;
imageBROKER 99cl / Günter Lenz 55cl /
Manfred Bail 100tl / Martin Siepmann 22–3c /
Petra Wallner 106crb; INTERFOTO 40clb, 44cb,
Schloss Nymphenburg *Lola Montez* (1847) by
J.K. Stieler 30cl, Munich City Museum/ *After
the assassination of Kurt Eisner February 21st
1919 in Munich* by Emanuel Bachrach-Bareé
41cla; Andrew Michael 31crb; OnTheRoad
35cr; peterforsberg 70tr; Prisma by Dukas
Presseagentur GmbH 42br; Prochasson
Frederic 103t; Peter Schickert 86–7; Robert
Haas / Süddeutsche Zeitung Photo 116tl;
122tr; Sueddeutsche Zeitung Photo /
Stephan Rumpf 58b, 109tl; Steve Vidler 112tl;
Westend61 GmbH / Martin Siepmann 74br.
Allianz Arena: B. Ducke 48bl. **Andechser:**
69br. **Artothek: Alte Pinakothek, Munich**
Battle of Alexander at Issus (1529) by Albrecht
Altdorfer 19tl, *Land of Cockaigne* (1566) by
Pieter Brueghel 18–19c, *Disrobing of Christ*
(c.1608) by El Greco 18cl, *Willem van
Heythuysen* (c.1625) by Frans Hals 19br, *The
Rape of the Daughters of Leucippus* (1618) by
Peter Paul Rubens photo Blauel/Gnamm
18br. **AWL Images:** Walter Bibikow 79br;
Cahir Davitt 72b; Stefano Politi Markovina 1.
Bavaria Filmstadt: 56t. **Bayerische
Staatsgemäldesammlungen, München:** Jens
Weber 45tr. **Bayerische Staatsoper:** Wilfried
Hösl *Alice Im Wunderland*-Choreographie
Christopher Wheeldon, Musik Joby Talbot,
Musikalische Leitung Myron Romanul 75tr.
**Bayerische Verwaltung der Staatlichen
Schlösser, Gärten und Seen:** 36cr, 36bl,
37cr; Dorling Kindersley/ Dorota Jarymowicz,
Mariusz Jarymowicz 16bl, 17crb.
Blutsgeschwister GmbH: 71clb, 85cl. **BMW
AG:** 32cl, 128tl. **Boulderwelt:** Tobias Leipnitz
48t. **Brasserie OskarMaria:** 94t.
Café Lotti: 61clb. **Chez Fritz:** 117cra.
Depositphotos Inc: DmitryRukhlenko 30–31c.
Deutsche Eiche: 59br. **Deutsches Museum:**
S. Wameser 26cla, 26cr, 26crb, 27tl, 28tr,
28bl, 29cl, 29b, 52tr, 119tr. **Courtesy Die Neue
Sammlung – The International Design
Museum Munich:** Rainer Viertlböck 20bl.
Doppler Shop: Sabine Doppler 115bc.
Dreamstime.com: Acrogame 67cla;
Rostislav Ageev 15cr, 88cla, 97b; Ahfotobox
111t; Anderm 50b; Annemario 47clb, 127tr;
Nedim Bajramovic 113cl; Beriliu 17tl; Bikemp
53cl; Carso80 120bl; Cyphix 89b; Yury
Dmitrienko 12cl; Electropower 12bl; Elenatur
37tl, 135b; Fottoo 23tl, 104tl; Glacyer 33tr,
41bl; GoranJakus 45bl; Gordzam 11tl; Diego
Grandi 122bl; Hitmans 23crb; Mapics 3tl,
76–7; Patrickwang 128br; Paulmz 66br; Denio
Rigacci 117c; Rosshelen | 95clb; Rudi1976 2tl,
8–9; Somchai Sinthop 4b; Jose Juan Pasarin
Vazquez 83cra; Whosegallery 132c; Yfwong74
16c; Yorgy67 134clb; Zaramira 72cl;
Zoom-zoom 4cra.
Erzbischofliches Odinariat Munich: Dorling
Kindersley/Pawel Wojcik 41tr. **EurArt:** 73tl.
FC Bayern Basketball: 120tr. **Ferdings GmbH:**
Stefan Herx 123crb. **Filmfest München:** 56bl.
Flushing Meadows: Chez Stefanie Franz: 2tr,
3tr, 4clb, 6cla, 7tl, 7cra, 10cr, 10clb, 10br, 11ca,
12–13c, 13cra, 14cra, 14clb, 14br, 14–15c, 15tr,
17cl, 22bl, 26tr, 30clb, 38–9, 40tc, 42t, 51clb,
57tr, 62c, 62br, 61br, 66tl, 66c, 68tl, 68c, 68br,
69br, 73br, 82clb, 89tr, 90b, 92bc, 93tl, 93crb,
100br, 101cla, 101cb, 103br, 104bl, 105cl, 107cl,
107br, 111br, 112bl,114tl, 114br, 121cl, 124tr,
124crb, 130br, 136t, 138–9.
Gärtnerplatztheater: Ida Zenna 4t; Anton
Brandl 81cl. **Gasteig:** 54t. **Vera Gaudermann:**
71tr. **Getty Images:** Hannes Magerstaedt 129cl;
Universal Images Group / Eye Ubiquitous
30crb. **Green City e.V:** Gleb Polovnykov 74cla.

HOFSTATT: 70bl, 85tr.

iStockphoto.com: argalis 46bl; Bankbuster 78cl; benedek 79cla; E+ / elkor 118tr; nedomacki 92tl.

Jüdisches Museum München: Roland Halbe 80tl.

Kilians Irish Pub: 84tl. **Kindermuseum München:** 52clb. **Kino am Olympiasee:** 32br, 57cl. **Kokolores:** Katrin Göbel 115tr.

La Kaz: 125b. **Livingroom:** Gerals Klepka 115cl. **Lollo Rosso:** 116br. **Löwenbräukeller:** Kerstin Jungblut 69cla.

Metropoltheater: Jakob Piloty 55tr. **Milch und Bar:** 84br. **MÜNCHEN MARATHON:** Norbert Wilhelmi 49tr. **Münchner Stadtmuseum:** 80bc. **Museum Brandhorst:** Sibylle Forster 21t, Haydar Koyupinar 21cl, 98br. **Museum Fu ünf Kontinente:** 112cb.

Olympiapark München: 4crb, 11cb, 32–3tc.

Pinakothek der Moderne: Massimo Fiorito 44t; Haydar Koyupinar 98t. **Prinz Myshkin:** 63tc, 63br, 83bc. **Julian Puttins:** 11clb, 34clb, 35tl.

Residenz Theater: Thomas Aurin 54bl. **Restaurant Tantris:** Christoph A. Hellhake 64bl. **Rote Sonne:** Südmotor GmbH, Bernd Bergmann/Christoph Ziegler 59cl. **Ruffini:** 131cr.

Sai Spa: Peter Hinze 49cl. **Stadtwerke München:** Kerstin Groh 33crb, 130tl. **Strom:** 58tl.

Tourist-Information Bad Tölz: 67br.

Vinothek by Geisel: Thomas Haberland 65cl. **Volkssternwarte München:** 50tl.

White Rabbit's Room: 65tr.

Zauberberg: Claudia Kimbacher 64tr. **Zuckertag:** 53tr.

Cover images:

Front and spine: **AWL Images:** Stefano Politi Markovina.

Back: **123RF.com:** filmfoto tr; **AWL Images:** Stefano Politi Markovina b; **iStockphoto.com:** Nikada tl, RudyBalasko cla, stockcam crb.

Pull out map cover image:

AWL Images: Stefano Politi Markovina.

For further information see:
www.dkimages.com

Illustrator Matthias Liesendahl.

Penguin
Random
House

First edition 2005

Published in Great Britain by
Dorling Kindersley Limited
DK, One Embassy Gardens, 8 Viaduct
Gardens, London SW11 7BW, UK

The authorised representative in the EEA is
Dorling Kindersley Verlag GmbH. Arnulfstr.
124, 80636 Munich, Germany

Published in the United States by
DK Publishing, 1745 Broadway, 20th Floor,
New York, NY 10019, USA

Copyright © 2005, 2023 Dorling
Kindersley Limited

A Penguin Random House Company

23 24 25 10 9 8 7 6 5 4 3 2

A CIP catalogue record is available
from the British Library.

A catalogue record for this book is available
from the Library of Congress.

ISSN 1479-344X

ISBN 978-0-2416-1248-4

Printed and bound in Malaysia

www.dk.com

*As a guide to abbreviations in visitor information
blocks:* **Adm** = admission charge; **D** = dinner;
L = lunch.

MIX
Paper | Supporting
responsible forestry
FSC™ C018179

This book was made with Forest
Stewardship Council™ certified
paper – one small step in DK's
commitment to a sustainable future.
**For more information go to
www.dk.com/our-green-pledge**

Phrase Book

In an Emergency

Where is the telephone?	Wo ist das Telefon?	voh ist duss tel-e-fon?
Help!	Hilfe!	hilf-uh
Please call a doctor	Bitte rufen Sie einen Arzt	bitt-uh roof'n zee ine-en artst
Please call the police	Bitte rufen Sie die Polizei	bitt-uh roof'n zee dee poli-tsy
Please call the fire brigade	Bitte rufen Sie die Feuerwehr	bitt-uh roof'n zee dee foyer-vayr
Stop!	Halt!	hult

Communication Essentials

Yes	Ja	yah
No	Nein	nine
Please	Bitte	bitt-uh
Thank you	Danke	dunk-uh
Excuse me	Verzeihung	fair-tsy-hoong
Hello (good day)	Grüß Gott	goot-en tahk
Hello	Grüß Gott	grooss got
Goodbye	Auf Wiedersehen	owf-veed-er-zay-ern
Good evening	Guten Abend	goot'n ahb'nt
Good night	Gute Nacht	goot-uh nukht
Until tomorrow	Bis morgen	biss morg'n
See you	Tschüss	chooss
See you	Servus	sayr voos
What is that?	Was ist das?	voss ist duss
Why?	Warum?	var-room
Where?	Wo?	voh
When?	Wann?	vunn
today	heute	hoyt-uh
tomorrow	morgen	morg'n
month	Monat	mohn-aht
night	Nacht	nukht
afternoon	Nachmittag	nahkh-mit-tahk
morning	Morgen	morg'n
year	Jahr	yar
there	dort	dort
here	hier	hear
week	Woche	vokh-uh
yesterday	gestern	gest'n
evening	Abend	ahb'nt

Useful Phrases

How are you? (informal)	Wie geht's?	vee gayts
Fine, thanks	Danke, es geht mir gut	dunk-uh, es gayt meer goot
Until later	Bis später	biss shpay-ter
Where is/are..?	Wo ist/sind...?	voh ist/sind
How far is it to...?	Wie weit ist es...?	vee vite ist ess
Do you speak English?	Sprechen Sie Englisch?	shpresh'n zee eng-glish
I don't understand	Ich verstehe nicht	ish fair-shtay-uh nisht
Could you speak more slowly?	Könnten Sie langsamer sprechen?	kurnt-en zee lung-zam-er shpresh'n

Useful Words

large	groß	grohss
small	klein	kline
hot	heiß	hyce
cold	kalt	kult
good	gut	goot
bad	böse/schlecht	burss-uh/shlesht
open	geöffnet	g'urff-nett
closed	geschlossen	g'shloss'n
left	links	links
right	rechts	reshts
straight ahead	geradeaus	g'rah-der-owss

Making a Telephone Call

I would like to make a phone call	Ich möchte telefonieren	ish mer-shtuh tel-e-fon-eer'n
I'll try again later	Ich versuche es später noch einmal	ish fair-zookh-uh es shpay-ter nokh ine-mull
Can I leave a message?	Kann ich eine Nachricht hinterlassen?	kan ish ine-uh nakh-risht hint-er-lahss-en
answerphone	Anrufbeantworter	an-roof-be-ahnt-vort-er
telephone card	Telefonkarte	tel-e-fohn-kart-uh
receiver	Hörer	hur-er
mobile	Handy	han-dee
engaged (busy)	besetzt	b'zetst
wrong number	falsche Verbindung	falsh-uh fair-bin-doong

Sightseeing

entrance ticket	Eintrittskarte	ine-tritz-kart-uh
cemetery	Friedhof	freed-hofe
train station	Bahnhof	barn-hofe
gallery	Galerie	gall-er-ree
information	Auskunft	owss-koonft
church	Kirche	keersh-uh
garden	Garten	gart'n
palace/castle	Palast/Schloss	pall-ast/shloss
place (square)	Platz	plats
bus stop	Haltestelle	hal-te-shtel-uh
free admission	Eintritt frei	ine-tritt fry

Shopping

Do you have?/ Is there..?	Gibt es...?	geept ess
How much does it cost?	Was kostet das?	voss kost't duss
When do you open/	Wann öffnen Sie?	vunn off'n zee
close?	schließen Sie?	shlees'n zee
this	das	duss
expensive	teuer	toy-er
cheap	preiswert	price-vurt
size	Größe	gruhs-uh
number	Nummer	noom-er
colour	Farbe	farb-uh
brown	braun	brown
black	schwarz	shvarts
red	rot	roht
blue	blau	blau
green	grün	groon
yellow	gelb	gelp

Types of Shop

chemist (pharmacy)	Apotheke	appo-tay-kuh
bank	Bank	bunk
market	Markt	markt
travel agency	Reisebüro	rye-zer-boo-roe
department store	Warenhaus	vahr'n-hows
chemist's, drugstore	Drogerie	droog-er-ree
hairdresser	Friseur	freezz-er
newspaper kiosk	Zeitungskiosk	tsytoongs-kee-osk
bookshop	Buchhandlung	bookh-hant-loong
bakery	Bäckerei	beck-er-eye
butcher	Metzgerei	mets-ger-eye
post office	Post	posst
shop/store	Geschäft/Laden	gush-eft/lard'n
photography shop	Photogeschäft	fo-to-gush-eft
clothes shop	Kleiderladen, Boutique	kly-der-lard'n boo-teek-uh

Staying in a Hotel

Do you have any vacancies?	Haben Sie noch Zimmer frei?	*harb'n zee nokh tsimm-er-fry*
with twin beds?	mit zwei Betten?	*mitt tsvy bett'n*
with a double bed?	mit einem Doppelbett?	*mitt ine'm dopp'l-bet*
with a bath?	mit Bad?	*mitt bart*
with a shower?	mit Dusche?	*mitt doosh-uh*
I have a reservation	Ich habe eine Reservierung	*ish harb-uh ine-uh rez-er-veer-oong*
key	Schlüssel	*shlooss'l*
porter	Pförtner	*pfert-ner*

Eating Out

Do you have a table for…?	Haben Sie einen Tisch für…?	*harb'n zee tish foor*
I would like to reserve a table	Ich möchte eine Reservierung machen	*ish mer-shtuh ine-uh rezer-veer-oong makh'n*
I'm a vegetarian	Ich bin Vegetarier	*ish bin vegg-er-tah-ree-er*
Waiter!	Herr Ober!	*hair oh-bare!*
The bill (check), please	Die Rechnung, bitte	*dee resh-noong bitt-uh*
breakfast	Frühstück	*froo-shtock*
lunch	Mittagessen	*mit-targ-ess'n*
dinner	Abendessen	*arb'nt-ess'n*
bottle	Flasche	*flush-uh*
dish of the day	Tagesgericht	*tahg-es-gur-isht*
main dish	Hauptgericht	*howpt-gur-isht*
dessert	Nachtisch	*nahkh-tish*
cup	Tasse	*tass-uh*
wine list	Weinkarte	*vine-kart-uh*
glass	Glas	*glars*
spoon	Löffel	*lerff'l*
fork	Gabel	*gahb'l*
teaspoon	Teelöffel	*tay-lerff'l*
knife	Messer	*mess-er*
starter (appetizer)	Vorspeise	*for-shpize-uh*
the bill	Rechnung	*resh-noong*
tip	Trinkgeld	*trink-gelt*
plate	Teller	*tell-er*

Menu Decoder

Apfel	*upf'l*	apple
Apfelsine	*upf'l-seen-uh*	orange
Aprikose	*upri-kawz-uh*	apricot
Artischocke	*arti-shokh-uh-*	artichoke
Aubergine	*or-ber-jeen-uh*	aubergine (eggplant)
Banane	*bar-narn-uh*	banana
Beefsteak	*beef-stayk*	steak
Bier	*beer*	beer
Bohnensuppe	*burn-en-zoop-uh*	bean soup
Bratkartoffeln	*brat-kar-toff'ln*	fried potatoes
Bratwurst	*brat-voorst*	fried sausage
Brezel	*bret-sell*	pretzel
Brot	*brot*	bread
Brühe	*bruh-uh*	broth
Butter	*boot-ter*	butter
Champignon	*shum-pin-yong*	mushroom
Currywurst	*kha-ree-voorst*	sausage with curry sauce
Ei	*eye*	egg
Eis	*ice*	ice/ ice cream
Ente	*ent-uh*	duck
Erdbeeren	*ayrt-beer'n*	strawberries
Fisch	*fish*	fish
Fleisch	*flysh*	meat
Forelle	*for-ell-uh*	trout
Gans	*ganns*	goose
gebraten	*g'braat'n*	fried
Geflügel	*g'floog'l*	poultry
gegrillt	*g'grilt*	grilled
gekocht	*g'kokht*	boiled
Gemüse	*g'mooz-uh*	vegetables
geräuchert	*g'rowk-ert*	smoked
Gulasch	*goo-lush*	goulash
Hähnchen (Hendl)	*haynsh'n*	chicken
Hering	*hair-ing*	herring
Himbeeren	*him-beer'n*	raspberries
Kaffee	*kaf-fay*	coffee
Kalbfleisch	*kalp-flysh*	veal
Kaninchen	*ka-neensh'n*	rabbit
Karotte	*car-ott-uh*	carrot
Kartoffelpüree	*kar-toff'l-poor-ay*	mashed potatoes
Käse	*kayz-uh*	cheese
Knoblauch	*k'nob-lowkh*	garlic
Knödel	*k'nerd'l*	dumpling
Kuchen	*kookh'n*	cake
Lachs	*lahkhs*	salmon
Leber	*lay-ber*	liver
Marmelade	*marmer-lard-uh*	marmalade, jam
Milch	*milsh*	milk
Mineralwasser	*minn-er-arl vuss-er*	mineral water
Nuss	*nooss*	nut
Öl	*erl*	oil
Olive	*o-leev-uh*	olive
Pfeffer	*pfeff-er*	pepper
Pfirsch	*pfir-sh*	peach
Pflaume	*pflow-me*	plum
Pommes frites	*pomm-fritt*	chips/ French fries
Rindfleisch	*rint-flysh*	beef
Rührei	*rhoo-er-eye*	scrambled eggs
Saft	*zuft*	juice
Salat	*zal-aat*	salad
Salz	*zults*	salt
Sauerkirschen	*zow-er-keersh'n*	cherries
Sauerkraut	*zow-er-krowt*	sauerkraut
Sekt	*zekt*	sparkling wine
Senf	*zenf*	mustard
scharf	*sharf*	spicy
Schlagsahne	*shlahgg-zarn-uh*	whipped cream
Schnitzel	*shnitz'l*	veal or pork cutlet
Schweinefleisch	*shvine-flysh*	pork
Semmel	*tsem-mel*	bread roll
Spargel	*shparg'l*	asparagus
Spiegelei	*shpeeg'l-eye*	fried egg
Spinat	*shpin-art*	spinach
Tee	*tay*	tea
Tomate	*tom-art-uh*	tomato
Wassermelone	*vuss-er-me-lohn-uh*	watermelon
Wein	*vine*	wine
Weintrauben	*vine-trowb'n*	grapes
Wiener Würstchen	*veen-er voorst-sh'n*	frankfurter
Zitrone	*tsi-trohn-uh*	lemon
Zucker	*tsook-er*	sugar
Zwiebel	*tsveeb'l*	onion

Numbers

0	null	*nool*
1	eins	*eye'ns*
2	zwei	*tsvy*
3	drei	*dry*
4	vier	*feer*
5	fünf	*foonf*
6	sechs	*zex*
7	sieben	*zeeb'n*
8	acht	*uhkht*
9	neun	*noyn*
10	zehn	*tsayn*
11	elf	*elf*
12	zwölf	*tsverlf*
13	dreizehn	*dry-tsayn*
14	vierzehn	*feer-tsayn*
15	fünfzehn	*foonf-tsayn*
16	sechzehn	*zex-tsayn*
17	siebzehn	*zeep-tsayn*
18	achtzehn	*uhkht-tsayn*
19	neunzehn	*noyn-tsayn*
20	zwanzig	*tsvunn-tsig*

Street Index